NAPOLEON'S ARMY

1807–1814, as Depicted in
the Prints of Aaron Martinet

NAPOLEON'S ARMY

1807–1814, as Depicted in
the Prints of Aaron Martinet

GUY C. DEMPSEY, JR.

ARMS AND
ARMOUR

For Nancy

Arms and Armour Press
A Cassell Imprint
Wellington House, 125 Strand, London WC2R 0BB.

Distributed in the USA by Sterling Publishing Co. Inc.,
387 Park Avenue South, New York, NY 10016-8810.

British Library Cataloguing-in-Publication Data:
a catalogue record for this book is available from the
British Library

ISBN 1-85409-347-9

Designed and edited by DAG Publications Ltd.
Designed by David Gibbons; edited by Michael Boxall.

Many of the Martinet prints in this book have been
reproduced with the kind permission of the Anne S. K. Brown
Military Collection, Brown University Library. The rest
are from the author's personal collection.

Printed and bound in Slovenia
by arrangement with Korotan Ljubljana d.o.o.

CONTENTS

INTRODUCTION

Most readers of this book have already seen some reproductions of the prints of Napoleonic military uniforms produced by the publishing house of Aaron Martinet because they are eminently decorative works which have been used frequently as illustrations in both specialised and general texts about the Napoleonic era. Nevertheless, very few individuals can identify Martinet prints as such on sight, and fewer still are alert to the iconographic and historical significance of this artwork. Their familiarity has bred indifference rather than contempt, but the result is that Martinet prints have generally been overlooked as a primary source for the study of French First Empire military uniforms.[1] This is most unfortunate, because careful study of the prints yields a vast wealth of accurate information about that subject.

The present study focuses on a particular series of hand-coloured line engravings published by Martinet which is entitled *Troupes Françaises* [*French Troops*]. There are almost four hundred different prints in a full set from the series, each depicting one or more soldiers from a particular regiment of Napoleon's army. The colour, style and detail of French military costume is captured in a unique fashion by these authentically contemporary works. Publisher Aaron Martinet was, above all else, a businessman and the success of his business required him to produce prints which faithfully represented their chosen subjects. In this case, his profit motive led to the creation of enduring primary source material.

This book is divided into six sections, plus appendixes. The first section combines a brief biography of Aaron Martinet with a brief history of his business. The second provides detailed information about the *Troupes Françaises* series of prints, including a discussion about the way they were produced. The third presents an analysis of the reliability of the prints as a primary source for the study of Napoleonic military uniforms. The fourth gives background information about the uniforms worn by Napoleon's armies, which is included for use in connection with the print reproductions and the commentaries on individual prints that form, respectively, the fifth and sixth sections of the book. The appendixes take the place of a standard index, since they consist of lists of prints in the *Troupes Françaises* series sorted in a variety of ways so that the reader can trace a particular print by means of any one of the following types of information: 1) the number indicating its order of appearance in the Martinet series; 2) the number indicating its order of appearance in this book; and 3) the type of military unit depicted in the print.

I. AARON MARTINET AND HIS BUSINESS

People have always been curious about the world around them and have explored many ways of communicating information to satisfy that curiosity. From the time of cave paintings onward, visual images have played an important role in that communications effort, but, prior to the invention of printing, such images were rarely accessible to a wide audience. The printing press changed this situation dramatically by making possible the inexpensive reproduction of multiple copies of the same picture. It also made possible the business of publishing and distributing prints. During the Directory, Consulate and First Empire of France, one of the most successful individuals in this business was the Parisian print publisher and seller, Aaron Martinet (1762–1841).

Printing was, to a great extent, a family business for Martinet. He was the son of François-Nicolas Martinet (1725–1804), an illustrator and engraver for the royal studio established by the Bourbon monarchs of France.[2] The elder Martinet was a prolific artist and among his masterworks are his signed prints for *L'Histoire Naturelle des Oiseaux* by George Louis Leclerc, comte de Buffon (1708–88), an important work of 18th-century ornithology.[3] It is certain that Aaron worked as an engraver on some of his father's projects, but no specific prints engraved by him have ever been identified. As it turned out, however, his special talent lay in commissioning, editing and publishing the works of others.

The French Revolution was such a momentous time of national and international upheaval that it is easy to forget that many Frenchmen spent the period simply carrying on their lives in very ordinary ways. In 1792, Aaron Martinet married Madeleine Suzanne Meirieu, the daughter of a rich merchant, and in short order the couple produced four children. The combination of his age and marital and family status probably explains why he did not join the armed forces (either voluntarily or involuntarily), but in any event he was left free to pursue a civilian profession. Sometime

early in the marriage the couple inherited some valuable properties from her father. The sale of this inheritance in early 1795 apparently provided Martinet with sufficient capital to open a print publishing and selling business of his own. He did so by renting the premises at 124 (later renumbered as 13 and 15) rue du Coq-Saint-Honoré on the right bank in Paris. (The street, whose name was commonly abbreviated as 'rue du Coq', was widened and renamed rue de Marengo in the late 19th century.) The location was in the heart of a district already renowned for a concentration of print makers and sellers.

The business founded by Martinet was based on his ability to co-ordinate on a large scale the different types of talent needed to produce a single print by the intaglio process, named for the Italian word for incising or engraving.[4] In this process, a mirror-image of a subject is manually engraved or chemically etched into the surface of a copper plate. Ink is then applied to the plate and after it is wiped off the flat surface, it remains in the engraved recesses. A sheet of damp paper is pressed against the plate with sufficient force to make contact with the ink in the grooves. The 'print' created in this manner is a mirror-image of the image on the engraved plate, and is therefore an exact black-and-white copy of the original subject image.

Although few details of Martinet's business are known with certainty, it seems that his approach to producing such prints in a commercially viable volume and price was to engage specialists for each step in the process. Martinet himself may have been the person who chose the subjects to be depicted, but the original subject images were created by artists commissioned by him from a pool of painters he assembled who were familiar with his requirements and able to work within specific cost and time constraints. The resulting original works of art were trans-ferred to printing plates by master engravers. The reproduction of copies from the plate involved still other craftsmen. Finally, the black-and-white prints from a particular plate were farmed out to water-colourists to be hand-coloured from specifications based on the original artwork. The finished prints were sold in Martinet's shop.

From the start, Martinet hoped to appeal to a wide range of customers, so his business produced prints covering a wide range of tra-ditional subjects, including natural history, architecture and current events. But it soon became especially renowned for the produc-tion of caricatures dealing with the fashions and manners of Parisian society. These were serious works of art (as opposed to mere car-toons) and were similar to those being created in the same period on the other side of the English Channel by such artists as Isaac and George Cruikshank, James Gillray, Thomas Rowlandson and the other English caricatur-ists of the late 18th and early 19th centuries.

By choosing popular subjects and pro-ducing high quality, but reasonably priced, prints, Martinet quickly attained favourable public notice. As early as 1800, one finds the local press singling out for praise a series of satirical prints published by him on the fash-ions of Paris: 'Do you want to know what passes for the latest fashion? Then, instead of consulting the *Journal des modes* or the prints displayed on the quays of the Seine, you should make a visit '*chez Martinet, libraire, rue du Coq-Saint-Honoré.*' There you will find a series of excellent satirical prints entitled "Fashions and Novelties" or "The Highest Good Taste".' The article concludes with the favourable pronouncement that Martinet's prints are as good as 'English caricatures'.[5]

In addition to social caricatures, Mar-tinet's inventory encompassed satirical prints focused on topics such as England's unceasing financial support for coalitions against France. A representative print of this type is the one entitled 'Francis II Being Paid by England for the Blood of his Subjects'.[6] Other prints of cur-rent events were more serious, such as por-traits of Pope Pius VII and of both of Napoleon's empresses. Although the Constitu-tion of 1804 included a provision regarding liberty of the press, publishers could be and were shut down, so it is not surprising to find that Martinet did not publish caricatures of Napoleon or of other political and military fig-ures of the day. On the other hand actors were fair game and the Martinet series depicting famous actors and their roles, which began in 1796 and which was entitled '*Petite galerie dra-matique*', eventually totalled 1,637 prints.

A key element of Martinet's popularity and prosperity was the success of his then novel marketing scheme for promoting the sale of his prints by displaying them promi-nently in the windows of his place of business. By encouraging 'window-shopping', Martinet created a cultural phenomenon of its time:

> The gorgeous window displays in modern stores barely elicit any attention from the passing crowd, which instead presses around the modest store front on rue du Coq. This boutique has regular visitors which have never set foot in its interior; they are content to examine through the window the beautiful items offered for their enjoyment, which include carica-tures and prints on subjects ranging from theatre costumes, to portraits of actors and musicians and to the uniforms of French and foreign troops. ... We know of one sophisticated person who holds the opinion that it is more pleasant to spend an hour looking into the windows of Martinet's boutique than it is to sit

through the presentation of a classic play by Molière.[7]

In an unusual case of art imitating life, one of the first prints produced in France by lithography was a work by Pierre Nolasque Bergeret which was commissioned by Aaron Martinet in 1805 to memorialise this development. The work is entitled *Les Musards de la rue du Coq* (*The Loiterers of Coq Street*). It depicts a crowd of elegantly dressed and coiffed men and women looking into the two large windows of his shop, which is identified by the sign *Martinet Libraire*.[8]

Martinet's business was apparently a financial as well as a critical success. The first indication of this is the fact that he was able to expand his operations in 1808 to occupy the adjoining premises.[9] The second sign is that his work attracted imitators who tried to produce similar, if not identical, prints. For instance, even a casual glance at the military prints produced by the publishing house of Basset during this period reveals that they are blatant, although inferior, copies of some of the prints from the series discussed in this volume.[10]

Martinet was even able to maintain this success (and his wealth) through the turmoil of Napoleon's two abdications and the two restorations of the Bourbons. An example of how he did so is provided by the 1814–16 re-cycling of altered states of many of his military prints into a new series of uniform prints depicting the forces of the Bourbon monarchy.[11] Martinet also tried to cash in on the Allied occupation by producing a set of 55 prints of foreign soldiers entitled *Galerie Militaire*.[12] As is often the case with contemporary commercial prints representing uniforms from other countries, the accuracy of these prints is sometimes laughable (for example, the print (No. 46) depicting an 'Irish Soldier').

In 1821, Martinet settled a dowry of 18,000 francs plus 8,000 books on his daughter,

Suzanne-Flore, the only one of his children to survive to adulthood. That same year she married Herménégilde-Honorat Hautecoeur, a bookseller who was one of Martinet's neighbours in the Rue du Coq. Three years later Martinet retired at the age of 64, handing over his firm to his daughter and son-in-law in return for an annual rent. Aaron Martinet died in 1841, two months after the death of his wife. Under the Hautecoeur name, the business he founded was to endure into the 20th century.

II. THE *TROUPES FRANÇAISES* SERIES

Given the importance of military affairs during the Napoleonic era, it is not at all surprising to find that Martinet eventually decided that military figures and scenes would also be popular, and hence profitable, subjects for reproduction. His most significant work in that regard was the *Troupes Françaises* series of prints depicting French soldiers which is the subject of this volume. Many salient aspects of the series are discussed in detail in different sub-sections below, but one particularly important point should always be kept in mind. Every image in the series falls into one of two categories – it is either a single-subject print or a multi-subject print.

A single-subject print is a unique work of art representing the soldiers of one specific Napoleonic military unit. A particular single-subject print usually (but not invariably) bears no resemblance to any other print in the series. A multi-subject print, on the other hand, is one that is identical in terms of composition, but not of its colours or caption, with other prints in the series which represent other, similarly uniformed units. The reason for this similarity is that all the multi-subject prints of a particular subject were in fact struck from the same state of a particular printing plate. However, the resulting black-and-white prints were then differentiated by variations in colouring and customisation of the print captions so that in the end each one has unique qualities. Theoretically, such multi-subject prints could have allowed Martinet to represent the uniforms of all the regiments of a particular service branch using impressions from a single plate (i.e., he could have used the same multi-subject print for all thirty Dragoon regiments). In practice, however, he introduced diversity (both in terms of composition and of military ranks represented) by employing different versions, or 'Types', of multi-subject prints at the same time within the relevant genre.[13] For example, Martinet published at least 84 different Dragoon prints using seven different Types of multi-subject print plus one single-subject print.

A. ARTISTS AND ENGRAVERS

Although it is certain that Martinet employed a number of artists to create the artwork on which the prints in the *Troupes Françaises* series were based, very little is known about these individuals. According to artistic convention, prints often bear signatures or other information about the artists and engravers who created them, but most of the Martinet prints are disappointing in that regard. Twelve prints (see, e.g., Print Nos. 38/62 and 33/120 and other prints of Imperial Guard figures) bear the signature of an artist named Maleuvre (including one bearing an apparent signature date of '1806' (Print No. 23/100 – Polish Light Horse of the Guard); three (see Print Nos. 133/59, 134/60.1 and 125/88) bear the single initial 'G'; two (see Print Nos. 151/187 and 152/188) have a caption stating that the image is 'by a Customs Service Employee'; and one (Print No. 2/248) bears the name or signature 'Godissart' and the signature date '1811'.[14] Based on other avail-

able information about the artists who worked with Martinet, it is probable that this last name refers to an artist named Godissart de Cari and that he was also the artist who contributed the artwork for the prints marked with the letter 'G'.[15] It is also probable that some other artists must have been involved in the series because there are many unsigned prints (see, e.g., any print dated '1807') in which the face of the primary figure is rendered in a distinctly different style from that used for the faces of the soldiers in the signed prints.

Even in cases where the name of an artist used by Martinet can be identified, no other information about these contributors can be readily obtained. There is no entry at all for Godissart de Cari in the classic French art reference source, Bénézit's *Dictionnaire*, and the only entry for Maleuvre is inconsistent with other known facts.[16] Given that the artist named Maleuvre who worked on the Martinet prints must have been alive and well at least until 1810 in order to have been able to observe the white-uniformed Carabiniers depicted in one of his signed prints, he is unlikely to be the same person as the Pierre Maleuvre (*b*.1740) noted in Bénézit, who is listed as having died in 1803. The 'official' anonymity of these individuals may reflect the fact that they were considered to be journeyman commercial illustrators rather than serious artists.

One bit of misinformation about the Martinet prints which recurs from time to time even in reputable reference works is that they are based on paintings by an artist named Pierre Martinet (1781–*c*.1845).[17] That individual was in fact a painter of military scenes working during the First Empire, but he was not related in any way to Aaron Martinet and he was not involved in the Martinet publishing business.[18] Moreover, there is not a shred of evidence to suggest that he was a contributor to the series.

The Hautecoeur article asserts unequivocally that at least a portion of the *Troupes Françaises* series was engraved by two individuals, one named Queverdo and the other named Pigeot.[19] Bénézit's work does contain an entry for one François Pigeot the Elder, a 19th-century engraver, but provides no details of his work. There is only one other piece of information about engraving to be found on the prints. The name 'Maleuvre' engraved on Print No. 57/295 is followed by the notation 'sculp.', an abbreviation of the Latin word for carved or engraved.[20] This term, typically used to indicate the engraver of a plate, does not appear on any other print examined by the author. Its presence may therefore indicate that Maleuvre was both the painter and engraver of the picture for that print, a circumstance so unusual that it was found to be worthy of special notation.

B. PRINT APPEARANCE AND FORMAT

There are four consistent features in the appearance of the prints from this series:

1. They are all printed on rectangular sheets of paper having roughly the same dimensions (ranging from 22.5cm to 24cm in height and from 15cm to 16.5cm in width).[21]
2. The printed image always appears in a box outlined with a thin black line, which itself is always within another box defined by the tell-tale impression from the printing plate – an inevitable by-product of the intaglio printing process.
3. Every print is marked with the printed heading *Troupes Françaises* in script above the box containing the printed image. (Although there is no obvious explanation for this peculiar phenomenon, the last letter of the heading is always printed in such a way that it appears to be an 'a'

instead of an 's', thereby making the last word appear to be '*Françaisea*'. The existence of this apparent error on an alleged Martinet print is an important guarantee of its authenticity.)
4. The prints all bear the address of the Martinet firm, which almost always is introduced with the words '*A Paris, chez Martinet, Libraire, . . .*'.

Apart from these attributes, the Martinet prints come in a bewildering array of different formats if one defines a 'format' to be a particular arrangement of information about the print around the pictorial image. The five locations where such information is typically found are (1) just above each of the top corners of the print; (2) just below each of the bottom corners; (3) below the caption. However, there is no single print on which information is found in all these locations at the same time. For instance, Print No. 7/88 (Hussar, 2nd Regiment) has the following format:

Upper left-hand corner – Martinet series number ('Pl. 88') (the abbreviation 'Pl.' = '*Planche*', the French word for 'Plate' or, more colloquially, 'Print')
Upper right-hand corner – printed date ('(1807)')
Lower left-hand corner – copyright notice ('*Dép. à la Bib. Imp.*')[1]
Lower right-hand corner – publisher's address ('*À Paris chez Martinet, Libraire, rue du Coq No. 15*')
Under caption – nothing [22]

The author has identified 23 distinct formats, but the true number is almost certainly larger than that, especially if one distinguishes between cases in which (1) both the 'Pl.' notation and the accompanying print number are hand-written; (2) the 'Pl.' is printed, but the number is hand-written; (3) both the 'Pl.' and the accompanying number are printed.

C. SERIES CHRONOLOGY

One of the most challenging aspects of analysing the *Troupes Françaises* prints is the difficulty of placing them in a definitive chronological context. The task is seemingly straight-forward because many of the prints bear a specific date, but the sequence in which prints are numbered has frequent anomalies. The only way to reconcile some of the more peculiar situations is to keep two points in mind. First, a Martinet print which was created in a particular year (e.g., 1807) and marked with that date might be reprinted in a later year (e.g., 1810) with the original printed date on the plate unchanged. Secondly, it seems probable that the numbering system used by Martinet was not adopted until late 1809 or early 1810, at which time series numbers were added by hand to prints in inventory which did not have them.

To judge by the evidence of the dates printed on some of the prints, the series was apparently produced in a number of different annual issuances beginning in 1807. One thus finds prints bearing the dates '(1807)', '(1808)' and '(1809)'. Significantly, none of the prints bearing those dates has a format which includes a printed 'Pl.' prompt for insertion of the number of the print in the series sequence. This omission suggests that prints were published in those years without any thought being given to whether they were part of a continuing series.[23] With 1809, however, a change is evident. There are only a very few prints marked with that date, and none at all with printed dates for any year subsequent to 1809, although occasionally a date is added by hand to the caption of a print. At the same time, the printed 'Pl.' begins to be a standard format feature.

Common sense also supports the proposition that it was not until some time in 1809

that Martinet decided to organise the series more systematically by numbering the different prints. If that were not the case (and the prints were numbered as they were published), the prints dated '1807' would be the lowest numbered ones, followed in unbroken ascending order by the prints dated '1808' and those few dated '1809'. In fact, of course, while that sequence is generally observed, it is broken in many places. For instance, Print Nos 42 and 43 are dated '1808', but Print No. 44 is dated '1807'. Another manifestation of the broken sequence phenomenon is provided by the instances where an undated print (such as Print No. 75/37 (Light Cavalry, Dragoon, 29th Regiment)) showing the post-1808 expansion address of the Martinet firm of Rue du Coq Nos 13 & 15 has a lower series number than a print dated '1807' (such as Print No. 73/79 (Light Cavalry, Dragoon, 25th Regiment)) which displays the pre-expansion address.

In terms of the print production sequence, the practice of numbering was probably adopted shortly after the creation of Print No. 143/106 (Dragoon of the Paris Guard), which is a single-subject print and which is the highest numbered print bearing the printed date of '(1809)'. This print was almost certainly not precisely the 106th print created in the series, but more likely received that number as a result of the expansion of the series in 1809 prior to the addition of the numbering system.

In addition to the three sub-groups of prints bearing printed dates, there is one other *tranche* of prints in the series that can be linked to a particular year. In 1811, Martinet made an impressive effort to ingratiate himself with Napoleon by publishing 45 of his prints of Imperial Guard subjects as a separate collection which was extravagantly entitled *Galerie des Enfants de Mars* (*Gallery of the Children of Mars* [the Roman God of War]).[24] The title page of a bound copy of this set in the Anne

Brown Collection includes a dedication to 'Her Majesty the Empress and Queen'.

It is also possible to make some deductions about the calendar year in which a particular print was printed, by using known information about the use of different types of multi-subject prints in the series. For instance, when Martinet first began to produce prints illustrating soldiers of French Mounted Chasseurs of the Line, he did so using the Type I multi-subject Chasseur print bearing the printed date of 1807.[25] In later years, however, he updated this basic print with another model, the Type II Chasseur prints, which represented a different style of uniform. Given this sequence of events, it is possible to conclude that a Type I Chasseur print of a trooper of the 7th Regiment of Chasseurs which bears the printed date '(1807)' was probably in fact printed in 1809 or earlier. On the other hand, any Type II print representing the 7th Chasseurs was probably physically printed in 1809 or later.

The last point to be made about the chronology of this series is that a print with a manuscript date in the caption was, for obvious reasons, almost certainly printed subsequent to that date. Thus Print No. 129/23.1 (Light Infantry, Chasseur, – Regiment, Voltigeur from 1806 to 1814) was undoubtedly printed after the 1814 fall of Napoleon. Moreover, since the print shows a light infantry voltigeur wearing a post-1812 style jacket, the manuscript date is misleading because it implies that the same uniform would have been worn in 1806 as well.

D. THE COLOURING PROCESS

As noted above, the prints from the series came off the printing press in an uncoloured, black-and-white form. A very few examples of black-and-white prints from the series still exist, but their rarity strongly suggests that the Troupes Françaises prints were almost always hand-coloured before they were sold. This conclusion is reinforced by the inclusion in the series of numerous Types of multi-subject prints which are typically distinguishable from one another only by way of different uniform colours. Without colouring, these multi-subject prints would make no sense.

The evidence of the prints themselves also suggests that there must have been a system in place to assure quality control over the colouring process because the primary colours are invariably consistent among different examples of the same print (i.e., examples of Print No 80/181 (Mounted Chasseur Officer, 6th Regiment) from different sets always depict a green uniform with yellow facings). It is possible that the colourists may have worked from the original painting used to create the relevant printing plate, but unless only a few colourists were involved, that would have been an impractical process. It seems more likely that the colourists worked from sample prints coloured and annotated by the artist.

The colourists seem to have been called upon to do two types of work. Most commonly, the task involved the straightforward application of transparent washes of colour to the correct portions of the black-and-white prints. The skill involved here seems to have been that of maintaining some transparency even in the application of dark colours so that the engraved lines of the print were still visible and provided a shading effect. A particularly good example of such successful colouring is provided by the uniform and saddlecloth of the figure in Print No. 152/188 (Imperial Customs Service, Mounted Brigade).

At other times the colourist was required to use opaque applications of colour. These were typically used for the purpose of obscuring details of the underlying engraving that were irrelevant to the uniform being illustrated in a particular multi-subject print. For example, the wavy lace trim around the lapels and collar of the figure in Print No. 26/217 (Officer of the Polish Lancers of the Guard in 1810) has been painted over for the version of that multi-subject print found in Print No. 28/252 (Officer of the Lancers of the Guard, 2nd Regiment). In other cases, the opaque colouring was used to effect a special modification of the printed image, amounting to an alternate state of the print, without changing the underlying engraving. This technique was used on many series prints produced after the Bourbon restorations to erase politically sensitive images such as a shako plate in the form of an imperial eagle. For instance the author owns a version of Print No. 54/61 (Imperial Guard, Sailor) with an entirely black shako.

E. SIZE OF THE SERIES

One of the most noteworthy features of the *Troupes Françaises* series is that every print bears a printed or hand-written number. Since these numbers are found consistently on the same print in different collections, the only logical conclusion is that they were added to the prints by the publisher. (Additional support for this conclusion is provided by the fact that other sets of Martinet costume prints also have internally consistent numbering.) Such numbers would have been useful for several administrative purposes, but it is also possible that Martinet may have adopted the practice of numbering his prints simply because he had discovered the eternal marketing truth that collectors are particularly inspired to expenditure by the urge to own all the items in a defined set of objects.

The only known comprehensive inventory of the prints contained in the series is the one which appears on pages 299–313 in Glasser and which is based on the numbered set of prints in the National Library in Paris. (Appendix C sets out a corrected and expanded version of this list.) According to this inventory, the full run of prints is numbered from 1 to 296 and, indeed, this author has never seen a print with a number that falls outside that range.[26]

This numbering does not, however, reflect the actual size of the run of prints in the series because many of the numbers appear on two or more different prints. When these duplicate number prints are separately counted, the size of the series increases dramatically to a total of at least 397 prints. (Unfortunately, the nature of the quirks in the series numbering system makes it impossible to be certain whether this number is a definitive tally because even more duplicate number prints may exist without having been detected.) This total breaks down as follows in terms of the types of units represented by the prints:

Staff	14 prints
Guard (all types)	62 prints
Heavy Cavalry (16 regiments)	35 prints
Dragoons (30 regiments)	84 prints
Chasseurs (31 regiments)	60 prints
Hussars (12 regiments)	28 prints
Lancers	12 prints
Line Infantry	31 prints
Light Infantry	10 prints
Artillery	3 prints
Auxiliaries	44 prints
Foreign	14 prints
TOTAL	397 prints

There are several possible explanations for the phenomenon of duplicate numbering in the series. The simplest cases are those provided by Martinet's frequent use of several different Types of multi-subject print. Whenever an existing Type of print in circulation was replaced by a new Type, the new one was invariably given the same number as the old.

In the most extreme case identified in the research for this book, there are three different Types of Hussar print which can appear as Print No. 8 (Hussar, 3rd Regiment).

Duplicate numbering also arises from the inclusion of different states of the same print in the series. Technically speaking, a new 'state' of a print is created every time the engraving plate is modified and new prints are struck from it. In the case of the *Troupes Françaises* series, Martinet was sufficiently concerned about the accuracy of his finished prints as to cause many plates to be modified as a consequence of the adoption of the 1812 Regulations (discussed at greater length in Section IV below). As a result, a number of the prints in the series exist in both an original state showing the classic French uniform jacket, which was cut so as to leave visible the front of the vest, and in a later state showing the 1812-style jacket, which was fastened across the stomach to the waist.[27] Both states of the print, however, always bear the same numerical designation. New states of certain prints were also created after the Bourbon Restorations. In particular, printed captions were removed from prints when they referred either to Napoleon (see, e.g., Print No. 1/180.1 [Napoleon Emperor and King]) or to his Imperial Guard (see, e.g., Print No. 50/238.1 [Ex-Guard Train in 1813]).

One final type of duplicate numbering is more difficult if not impossible to explain. For instance, the prints in the series depicting soldiers from the regiments of Light Horse Lancers of the Line, which obviously could not have been added before that type of cavalry unit was created in 1811, have for the most part been assigned numbers already used for other, earlier prints. Hence, although there is a total of twelve prints of Lancers in the series, only three of them (Nos. 282, 283 and 284) bear numbers that are not shared on other prints. (See Appendix J for a full list of Lancer prints.) This result would be logical if Martinet were re-using numbers that were no longer needed in the series, which would have been the case if the Lancer prints had been assigned the numbers previously used for prints of those Dragoon regiments disbanded to form the Lancers, but the actual pairings do not seem to follow any such pattern.

III. RELIABILITY OF THE PRINTS

In order for Martinet's prints (or, for that matter, any pictures) to qualify as a primary source for the study of Napoleonic military uniforms, they must possess two key attributes: they must have been created during the Napoleonic era and they must be the product of first-hand observation of the uniforms depicted.

Given the dates on the works themselves and the histories both of the units illustrated and of Aaron Martinet's publishing business, the prints of the *Troupes Françaises* series undeniably possess the first attribute. The question of whether they also possess the second is more complex. In the end, it requires a two-part answer which differentiates between single-subject and multi-subject prints and demonstrates yet again the importance of taking a critical look at all source material.

Single-subject prints are highly reliable sources of information because there is a strong probability that they are based on artwork arising from direct contact between Martinet's artists and the soldiers they painted. On the other hand, the reliability of multi-subject prints varies significantly. At best, a particular version of a multi-subject print can have the same accuracy as a single-subject print, and can be very accurate for specific unit distinctions, but it cannot be relied upon as a primary source because of the lack of a proven connection between the artists and the subjects depicted. It can be accurate in a generic sense, that is to say it may be a reliable depiction of a typical soldier of the relevant type, but not necessarily what a particular soldier of a particular unit looked like.

A general point relevant to the assessment of the reliability of these prints needs to be discussed. This work refers to the possibility of the Martinet prints being a 'primary' source of information. Strictly speaking, of course, no print can have that status because a print is, inevitably, a derivative work produced by a printing plate which is, at best, only a copy of other artwork. It is that other artwork which is the true source of information. But this distinction is not important if the production process for the prints was such that the finished engraving looks the same as the original artwork in all material respects and, for the *Troupes Françaises* series, there happens to exist persuasive evidence that this was indeed the case. That evidence is provided by thirty-one of the original paintings for the series which can be found in the Brunon Collection housed in the *Château de l'Emperi* branch of the French Army Museum.[28]

These paintings (apparently watercolours) are unsigned, but most do have manuscript numbers and/or other annotations. The reason why they can be classified as the original artwork for the prints rather than manuscript copies is that the paintings sometimes contain details which are not found in the prints. For instance, the painting of an aide-de-camp which is the basis for the multisubject plate used to produce Print No. 4/272.1 (Aide-de-Camp of Mestre de Camp) contains the rather gory detail of a severed hand on the ground next to an abandoned pistol. In the finished print, only the pistol appears. The mounted figure in the print, however, is identical with that in the painting

except for the immaterial difference that he is wearing a *Légion d'honneur* decoration which is missing in the original artwork. This relationship holds for all the specimens examined.

A. SINGLE-SUBJECT PRINTS

The case for the accuracy of the single-subject prints in the series rests on one concrete piece of information, a bit of logic and a lot of circumstantial evidence. The concrete information is provided by the two prints (Nos. 151/185 and 152/186) which depict the uniforms of Napoleon's Customs Service. As noted earlier, each of these prints bears the notation that it was created by 'an employee of the Customs Service'. Assuming this statement is true (and there is no reason to believe that it is not), it is undeniable that the artist was personally familiar with his subjects and that the prints therefore constitute primary source material. Logic now comes into play. If Martinet as a publisher went to the trouble of commissioning a specialist artist to ensure the reliability of the illustrations of an obscure type of uniform, it seems reasonable to believe he would have made at least as much effort to ensure the accuracy of the other prints as well.

This belief is consistent with, and supported by, an impressive amount of circumstantial evidence. First, we know that the artists who worked on the series were professionals who possessed all the skills necessary to reproduce accurately any subject they desired. Second, these artists lived in Paris and, with very few exceptions, every uniform depicted in the series could have been seen in that city. (The large number of prints of Imperial Guard and Paris Guard figures emphasises that geographic reality.) Third, the artists depended on Martinet for continuing commissions, so they must have been highly motivated to provide a quality picture in response to every assignment. Martinet's artists therefore had the talent, opportunity and motivation necessary to make their single- subject prints highly reliable.

The desire for accuracy would have been equally shared by the publisher. To be successful, Martinet had to produce prints that people would buy, and the largest market by far for this artwork was undoubtedly provided by the soldiers of Napoleon's armies and their families. For the ordinary conscript who could not afford a portrait miniature, one of these prints was the best way to convey to his family an authentic image of his military appearance.[29] From the family's point of view, they could imagine the face of their missing loved one in place of that provided by Martinet's artists. Both these groups would have had a tendency to be intolerant of inaccurate pictures. In this context, errors might have translated into reduced print sales.

There is one final piece of negative evidence which completes the case for the accuracy of the single-subject prints in the *Troupes Françaises* series. If the prints are not the product of direct observation of the relevant troops by Martinet's artists, it is impossible to explain why there are so many cases in which the uniform information they contain is almost perfectly correlated with other primary source information that is now, but which was not necessarily then, available about the relevant dress. There was simply not enough accurate contemporary information about French uniforms readily available in Napoleonic Europe to have permitted Martinet's artists to work exclusively, or even primarily, from second-hand sources.[30] This point is highlighted by the number of instances in which a Martinet print is the only contemporary source of iconographic information about a particular military unit (see, e.g., the prints of the Customs Service, the Isembourg Regiment, the Lancer Gendarmes and the Volunteers of the Seine).

B. MULTI-SUBJECT PRINTS

As noted above, the reliability of the multi-subject prints in the *Troupes Françaises* series is variable: some are very reliable, some are moderately reliable and some cannot be considered reliable at all. The key factor in determining the degree of reliability is the extent to which the relevant print actually represents a subject which was observed by the relevant artist.

1. The following three kinds of multi-subject prints can, in whole or in part, be just as reliable as a single-subject print:

a. An 'Original Version' print is the version within a particular Type of multi-subject print that is identical with the artwork on which the Type is based. In other words, the Original Version for each print Type is the one that illustrates the unit which was actually observed by Martinet's artists. If that Original Version can be identified (which is not always possible), it is likely to be highly reliable because it was, *de facto*, a single-subject print until further prints were struck from the same plate. The Original Version therefore has the same reliability as any other single-subject print. This situation can be illustrated by reference to the Type I multi-subject prints of Polish Lancers which are scattered throughout the series (see Print Nos 24/205.1, 27/251, and 159/279). Because the Polish Lancers of the Guard were the first unit of that type to be added to the French Army (and to be available for viewing by Martinet's artists), it is likely that Print No. 24/205.1 is the Original Version in this multi-subject print series.

b. A 'Single Unit' print is a multi-subject print that is used only to illustrate soldiers of a single military unit or rank. Examples are the three prints of aides-de-camp (Print Nos. 220, 272 and 274) and the two prints of infantrymen of the Portuguese Legion (Print Nos 226 and 160/227). Since the basic uniform of all such figures was bound by regulation to be the same, with only details changing from version to version, these prints possess a high degree of accuracy and reliability even if the Original Version cannot be identified.

c. A 'Customised' print is a multi-subject print that has been extensively modified in the colouring process to alter the style of dress depicted (in addition to changes in colour). In such a print the relevant version has, in effect, been used simply as the foundation for a new piece of original artwork. A good example of a Customised print is Print No. 78/73.1 (Mounted Chasseur, 3rd Regiment), in which both the head-dress and jacket have been completely re-worked. Such significant intentional changes strongly suggest an intention to convey the results of direct eye-witness observation of the military unit represented.

2. The majority of all multi-subject prints fall into the category of being moderately reliable. Even in cases where the Original Version print for a Type cannot be identified (as is the case for all types of Cuirassier and Dragoon prints), it is nevertheless likely that each Type of multi-subject print does in fact reflect the occurrence of at least one direct contact between a Martinet artist and the relevant subject, and the prints can be considered to be generically accurate as to the uniforms depicted. So, for example, each Dragoon print illustrates a uniform that could have been worn during the period of 1807–14 by the regiment or unit represented, but there is no way of knowing whether it was a uniform that was definitely worn by that group at any particular time.

3. There are two kinds of multi-subject print that are less reliable than all the others.

a. A 'Secondary Version' print is any of the other versions in a Type for which an Original Version print has been identified. For instance, using the example of the Type I Polish Lancer prints discussed in Section III(B)(1)(a) above, any print of that Type that does not depict a Polish Lancer of the Guard is a Secondary Version print. Any Secondary Version Print is likely to be less reliable than the Original Version because it is adapted from the Original Version rather than created from original artwork. However, to the extent that (1) the uniforms for those other units were, in fact, identical in style with that depicted in the Original Version print, and/or (2) the colourist was able to replicate any known differences in the course of the colouring process, a Secondary Version print can still provide reliable information. Using these criteria, one can conclude that the Secondary Version print of the Dutch Lancers of the Guard is reasonably reliable because of the prescribed similarities between the style of the uniforms of that unit and the style of the uniforms of the Polish Lancers, while the Secondary Version print of the Vistula Legion Lancers has material inaccuracies, probably because the unit was never directly observed by the relevant artist.

b. A 'Multi-nationality' print is any print in a Type that is used to represent uniforms of more than one nation. The only known example of this kind of print in the series is Print No. 147/127.1 (Battalion of Chasseurs, residing at Flushing). The basic image used is the same as that used for the Berg Line Infantry (Print Nos. 19.1 and 20.2) and for the Neufchâtel Battalion in Martinet's series of prints on foreign units and uniforms. Because there is no independent proof that the uniforms of these three very different units looked alike, this print must be considered unreliable as to style. For separate reasons (probably related to the fact that it is unlikely that any soldiers from this unit were ever present in Paris), it also seems that the uniform colours for the Flushing Chasseurs presented in this print are inaccurate. Martinet's print follows the 1802 decree that created the unit in depicting an iron-grey uniform with blue collar and cuffs, but a recent article about the dress of the Chasseurs uses archival sources to determine that the uniform was more likely sky-blue with dark blue collar, cuffs and lapels.[31] The article also quotes contemporary reports as stating that the unit was poorly equipped and uniformed, facts at odds with a depiction showing a figure from the unit wearing a shako with full dress cords and a plume.

IV. UNIFORM INFORMATION

The bulk of this book is devoted to reproductions of individual prints from the *Troupes Françaises* series and related commentaries. The purpose of this section is to set the stage for those sections by providing some general information about the prints and about French Napoleonic military uniforms. Most of the uniform information in this section comes from the 'official' regulations describing the dress of the French army during the Napoleonic era. This type of primary source information, while not always reliable when considered in isolation, is particularly useful for comparison and contrast with the uniform information provided by the Martinet prints.

The only comprehensive uniform regulations adopted during Napoleon's reign were the Imperial Decree of 19 January 1812 'Relating to Infantry Uniforms' and the companion Decree of 7 February 1812 'Relating to Cavalry Uniforms'.[32] These regulations (hereinafter referred to as the '1812 Regulations'), which prescribe in detail the size, shape and colours of the uniforms for all the different types of mounted and dismounted troops in the French regular army, probably did not have any practical effect on military dress until the massive re-uniforming which took place in early 1813. Before then, although many new units created by Napoleon were covered by specific uniform decrees, there were no general dress regulations in place for the cavalry, and the only ones Napoleon promulgated for his infantry were the decree of 25 February 1806 making the shako a general issue item in place of the hat,[33] and the short-lived regulation of 25 April 1806 (hereinafter referred to as the 'White Uniform Regulation') which attempted to change the basic colour of French infantry uniforms from blue to white.[34]

As a consequence of these circumstances, the 'official' information about the military dress depicted by Martinet from 1807–12 has come for the most part from the uniform descriptions contained in the government-sponsored *État Militaire* [Military Yearbook] for Year X [1801–2].[35] This source provides detailed information about uniform colours, but relatively little about styles. In terms of pre-1812 head-dress, equipment and accoutrements, the best information comes from the '1801 Equipment Specifications' dated 4 *Brumaire* Year X (26 October1801) which sets out the dimensions and price of all 'effects' (ranging from cartridge boxes to dragoon helmets) which had to be purchased with regimental funds.[36]

The information in this section is arranged in twelve subsections which anticipate the arrangement of the reproductions in accordance with the twelve most significant categories of unit which comprised the army of Napoleon.

A. STAFF

The dress of French generals and the various types of officer attached to the general staff was the subject of the comprehensive 'Staff Dress Regulations' dated 1 *Vendémiaire* Year XII (24 September 1803) which remained officially in effect until the adoption of the 1812 Regulations, but unofficially probably lasted even longer than that. The full title of the Year XII document was 'Regulation of the uniforms of generals, of army and garrison staff officers, of officers of the corps of engineers, of inspectors of reviews, of war commissaries, of reformed officers, of retired officers, of medical officers and of members of the administration of military hospitals.' The Staff Dress Regulations even included an extensive series of plates illustrating in detail the different types of braid and lace contemplated, and the appearance of many other items of dress and equipment. The Staff Dress Regulations were published in *Journal Militaire* for Year XII (Pt. 2).

The prints of Staff subjects are all single-subject except for the aide-de-camp prints which are highly reliable Single-Unit prints.

B. IMPERIAL GUARD CAVALRY

The dress of most of Napoleon's Imperial Guard cavalry regiments is well-known in general, but the Martinet prints provide many details that are not available elsewhere. The prints dealing with these units are single-subject with only the following exceptions:

Type I Polish Lancer – Mounted lancer carrying lance. This is an Original Version print.

Type II Polish Lancer – Lancer officer brandishing sword. This too is an Original Version print.

Type I Honour Guard – Mounted Honour Guard trooper looking towards the rear. This is a Single-Unit print.

Type I Chasseur – Dismounted Chasseur trooper in ordinary dress. This is probably a generically reliable multi-subject print.

C. IMPERIAL GUARD INFANTRY

The most convenient source of accurate information about Imperial Guard uniforms is Louis Fallou's exceptional work, *La Garde Impériale* (Paris, 1901; Krefeld, 1975) (hereinafter referred to as 'Fallou'). Fallou's work is technically only a secondary source, but it presents an extraordinary compilation of primary iconographic and documentary information about the organisation and uniforms of Napoleon's Guard. Its only defect is a lack of source citations.

The only multi-subject print dealing with Guard infantry is the one used to represent a number of different Middle and Young Guard units such as the Tirailleurs and Voltigeurs. This Type I Tirailleur print (which is a generically reliable print) shows an infantryman advancing with fixed bayonet wearing a shako, a light Infantry-style jacket with short tails and breeches. Details of the uniforms of these various units (as specified in Fallou) were:

Regiment	Lapels	Collar	Cuffs	Cuff Flap	Pocket
Tirailleur-Grenadiers (1809)	blue	scarlet	scarlet	none	vertical

Details: Red plume and white cords for shako; red shoulder-straps; blue eagle ornaments in turnbacks.

Conscript-Grenadiers (1809)	blue	blue	scarlet	white	not known

Details: White chevron, red plume and cords on shako; square, line infantry-style lapels; blue swallow's nest epaulets trimmed red; white turnbacks with red eagle ornaments.

Tirailleurs (1810)	blue	scarlet	scarlet	none	vertical

Details: Red plume and cords for shako; red shoulder-straps piped white; blue eagle ornaments in turnbacks.

Tirailleur-Chasseurs (1809)	blue	blue	scarlet	none	vertical

Details: Green plume and white cords; green shoulder-straps piped white; green eagle and hunting-horn ornaments alternating in blue turnbacks.

Conscript-Chasseurs (1809)	blue	red	red	none	not known

Details: White chevron and cords on shako; green, pear-shaped pompom; green swallow's nest epaulets trimmed red; blue turnbacks with green hunting horn ornaments; blue vest and trousers.

Voltigeurs (1810)	blue	yellow	scarlet	none	vertical

Details: Green plume and white cords; green shoulder-straps piped white; green eagle and hunting-horn ornaments alternating in blue turnbacks.

National Guards (1810)	white	scarlet	scarlet	none	not known

Details: Cords, pompom and plume for shako varied according to type of company: Grenadiers – red, Voltigeurs – green, Fusiliers – white cords and pompoms and plumes according to company colour; white turnbacks with red grenade and red epaulets for Grenadiers; green horns and epaulets for Voltigeurs; blue eagles and blue swallow's nests piped red for Fusiliers.

D. IMPERIAL GUARD SUPPORT TROOPS

These units are covered in Fallou's work. The only multi-subject print involved is that which is used for both the dismounted Horse Artilleryman and the dismounted Chasseur.

E. CARABINIERS AND CUIRASSIERS

1. Carabiniers

The prints illustrating Carabinier uniforms (both before and after the uniform change of 1810–11) form an odd exception to some of the rules of reliability as applied to the Troupes Françaises series. The oddity is that they are essentially single-subject and multi-subject simultaneously because the only dress distinction between the two Carabinier regiments was a difference in cuff colour. They are all, however, very reliable.

2. Cuirassiers

The subject of Cuirassier uniforms is very complex because this branch of service went through a number of different styles of dress during the Napoleonic period. The best single treatment of the topic is Commandant E.-L. Bucquoy's monograph *Les Cuirassiers 1800– 1815* (Troyes, 1934) (hereinafter referred to as 'Bucquoy').

The Martinet series includes the following four different types of Cuirassier multi-subject print, all of which are generically reliable:

TYPE I – Mounted Cuirassier trooper dated 1808. This is the weakest print in the series from the point of view of artistic technique. The basic shape and colour of the helmet and breast plate are sound, but all the fine points such as the cuirass lining, the plate bolts and the shoulder-strap are poorly defined. The horse furniture is better drawn, and it is interesting to see that the artist has chosen a model that does not include a sheepskin saddle cover. The sabre hilt is significantly inaccurate.

TYPE II – Mounted Cuirassier trooper. This is simply an improved version of the Type I prints and it adds such details as a proper cuirass liner, a corrected sabre hilt and a white sheepskin saddle cover. The helmet has the type of rakish styling which became popular post-1811.

TYPE III – Mounted Cuirassier Superior Officer brandishing his sword. A generally sound generic print, although both the sabre and scabbard seem a bit thin and the shape of the shoulder-strap is still inaccurate. The only Cuirassier officers with

CUIRASSIER FACING COLOURS

Regiment		Collar	Cuffs	Cuff Flap	Pocket
1	(Year X)	scarlet	scarlet	scarlet	horizontal
	(1812)	”	”	”	vertical
2	(Year X)	blue	scarlet	blue	horizontal
	(1812)	scarlet	scarlet	”	vertical
3	(Year X)	scarlet	blue	scarlet	horizontal
	(1812)	”	”	”	vertical
4	(Year X)	scarlet	scarlet	scarlet	vertical
	(1812)	aurore	aurore	aurore	”
5	(Year X)	blue	scarlet	blue	vertical
	(1812)	aurore	aurore	”	”
6	(Year X)	scarlet	blue	scarlet	vertical
	(1812)	aurore	”	aurore	”
7	(Year X)	yellow	yellow	yellow	horizontal
	(1812)	”	”	”	vertical
8	(Year X)	blue	yellow	blue	horizontal
	(1812)	yellow	”	”	vertical
9	(Year X)	yellow	blue	yellow	horizontal
	(1812)	”	”	”	vertical
10	(Year X)	yellow	yellow	yellow	vertical
	(1812)	rose	rose	rose	”
11	(Year X)	blue	yellow	blue	vertical
	(1812)	rose	rose	”	”
12	(Year X)	yellow	blue	yellow	vertical
	(1812)	rose	”	rose	”
13	(1812)	wine	wine	wine	vertical
14	(1812)	wine	wine	blue	vertical

two rows of lace on their horse furniture were Colonels and Lieutenant-colonels.

TYPE IV – Mounted Cuirassier Trumpeter blowing trumpet. The quality of this print is excellent except that the size of the trumpet is possibly exaggerated.

The facing colours prescribed for the different Cuirassier regiments in (1) the Military Year-book for Year X (except where otherwise noted) and (2) the 1812 Regulations were as shown in the table on the facing page.

F. DRAGOONS

The green coats and brass helmets of Napoleon's Dragoons were a common sight on all the battlefields of the First Empire, but there has never been a serious study of the dress of this branch of French cavalry. The best general treatment of the subject is provided by the five different plates devoted to Dragoons by Lucien Rousselot (Plate Nos 7, 20, 25, 86 and 96).

The Martinet series includes the following seven different types of Dragoon multi-subject prints, all of which are generically reliable:

TYPE I – Mounted Dragoon trooper in profile dated 1807. This is a very accurate depiction of the classic First Empire Dragoon uniform. The black shape on top of the folded cloak behind the rider is probably intended to suggest a part of the cartridge box. The unusual shape of the sabre hilt suggests that the print was drawn by the same artist who created the Type I Cuirassier print. This is the only print in the series that depicts a riding-boot with a visible knee cuff.

TYPE II – Dragoon trooper, dismounted beside his horse, pulling on gauntlets. The jacket cuff is very clearly seen in this composition.

TYPE III – Dragoon galloping with captured English regimental standard. The uniform and accoutrements of a typical Napoleonic Dragoon are very clearly depicted.

TYPE IV – Mounted Dragoon Officer. In this generic print Type, the officer has two fringed epaulettes, so the artist must have had either a squadron commander or a major in mind; the latter is the more likely possibly because white plumes were normally reserved for members of the regimental staff. The details of the uniform and equipment are classic and non-controversial except for the triple flaps on the holster cover, which are a feature found only in Martinet Dragoon prints. The silver trim on the cuff of the gauntlet is an exotic touch.

TYPE V – Mounted Elite Company trooper brandishing sabre. The angular shape of the holster covers is unique to these Type IV Dragoon prints.

TYPE VI – Mounted Dragoon Colonel with sword dangling from wrist-strap. The unusual shape of the sabre guard probably results from a failed attempt to represent the metal work in the shape of a scallop shell which was common on Dragoon officers' weapons.

TYPE VII – Mounted Dragoon paying court to woman in window. The print is interesting for its uniform and non-uniform details alike.

This selection of Types is unusual because it very broad, yet it does not include any trumpeter or musician figures. The facing colours prescribed for the different Dragoon regiments in (1) the Military Yearbook for Year X (except where otherwise noted) and (2) the 1812 Regulations were as follows (only one set of details is given if both sources are in agreement):

DRAGOON FACING COLOURS

Regiment		Lapels	Collar	Cuffs	Cuff Flap	Pocket
1		scarlet	scarlet	scarlet	scarlet	horizontal
2	(VIII)	scarlet	green	scarlet	scarlet	horizontal
	(1812)	"	"	"	green	"
3	(XI)	scarlet	green	green	scarlet	vertical
	(1812)	"	scarlet	"	"	horizontal
4		scarlet	scarlet	scarlet	scarlet	vertical
5		scarlet	green	scarlet	green	vertical
6		scarlet	scarlet	green	scarlet	vertical
7		crimson	crimson	crimson	crimson	horizontal
8		crimson	green	crimson	green	horizontal
9	(X)	[no description]				
	(1812)	crimson	crimson	green	crimson	horizontal
10		crimson	crimson	crimson	crimson	vertical
11	(VIII)	crimson	green	crimson	[not shown]	vertical
	(1812)	"	"	"	green	"
12		crimson	crimson	green	crimson	vertical
13		dark pink	dark pink	dark pink	dark pink	horizontal
14		dark pink	green	dark pink	green	horizontal
15		dark pink	dark pink	green	dark pink	horizontal
16		dark pink	dark pink	dark pink	dark pink	vertical
17		dark pink	green	dark pink	green	vertical
18		dark pink	dark pink	green	dark pink	vertical
19		jonquil	jonquil	jonquil	jonquil	horizontal
20		jonquil	green	jonquil	green	horizontal
21	(XI)	jonquil	jonquil	green	jonquil	horizontal
22	(1812)	jonquil	jonquil	jonquil	jonquil	vertical
23	(1812)	jonquil	green	jonquil	green	vertical
24	(1812)	jonquil	jonquil	green	jonquil	vertical
25	(1812)	aurore	aurore	aurore	aurore	horizontal
26	(1812)	aurore	green	aurore	green	horizontal
27	(1812)	aurore	aurore	green	aurore	horizontal
28	(1812)	aurore	aurore	aurore	aurore	vertical
29	(1812)	aurore	green	aurore	green	vertical
30	(1812)	aurore	aurore	green	aurore	vertical

G. MOUNTED CHASSEURS

Line Chasseur uniforms were always predominantly green, but their style changed several times during the Napoleonic era. These styles were distinguished primarily by the type of jacket worn and, in roughly chronological order of appearance, they were as follows:

1. Dolman (usually with three vertical rows of buttons) and barrel sash, but no pelisse.

2. Jacket with long tails and pointed lapels.
3. Single-breasted jacket with short tails (or 'Kinski' jacket).
4. Jacket with short tails and lapels closed to the waist.

Since the timing of clothing changes varied from regiment to regiment, there was always a number of different styles in use at the same time. For instance, the figures illustrated in the Otto Manuscript, which dates to 1807, include a Chasseur of the 5th Regiment wearing a dolman, one of the 24th wearing a Kinski jacket and one of the 26th Chasseurs wearing a long jacket with pointed lapels.[37] The best modern summary of information on Chasseur uniforms can be found in a pair of articles by Rigo: 'Les Chasseurs à Cheval de la Ligne, Première Epoque 1801–1808' and 'Les Chasseurs à Cheval de la Ligne, Deuxième Epoque 1809–1815', in *Uniformes*, No. 36 (March–April 1977), pp. 30–6 ('Regs I'), and No. 37 (May–June 1977), pp. 15–19 ('Regs II').

The Martinet series includes the following three different types of Chasseur multi-subject print which together illustrate three of the four main styles of Chasseur dress:

TYPE I – Mounted Chasseur in a dolman with barrel sash and hussar-style breeches, dated 1807. The dolman has three vertical rows of buttons, which seems to have been the norm, but there are many surviving examples of Chasseur dolmans with five rows.[38] In the standard state of this print, the Chasseur is wearing a shako with a plume, white cords, white metal chin scales and a white metal, diamond-shaped plate decorated with an eagle. There is a white line on the breeches of each figure just under the right forearm which is difficult to place in context, although it may simply be intended to be a portion of the

Austrian knot or spear-head decoration which would typically be found on the front of the thigh of such trousers. This print provides an exceptionally accurate depiction of the manner in which the carbine was suspended, muzzle down from a metal clip attached to the shoulder-belt. In many versions of this print, the colour black is applied so heavily to the boots that the left and right feet of the figure are not separately distinguishable.

TYPE II – Mounted Chasseur trooper wearing a single-breasted Kinski jacket and a shako with a small rear visor. This is one of the most puzzling figures in the series because no other source, primary or secondary, associates a second visor of this sort with any type of French Napoleonic shako. (The feature is, in fact, only known to have been used on Light Horse Lancer helmets. See Section IV (H) below.) The feature is mentioned without comment by Rousselot in his Plate No. 11: *Chasseurs à Cheval – Généralités*, and it is not discussed at all in Christian Blondeau's encyclopedic work on Napoleonic shakos. Another unusual feature is the odd turnback ornament in the form of a strip of green lace held in place by two silver buttons.

TYPE III – Mounted Chasseur officer (either a captain or a lieutenant) in a hybrid outfit which combines a single-breasted Kinski jacket with hussar-style breeches with lace trim. This combination suggests a date of 1809 for the picture. The print accurately depicts the fashion among junior Chasseur officers to do away with the counter-epaulettes on the right shoulder which would otherwise be part of their normal insignia of rank.

The facing colours prescribed for the different Chasseur regiments in (1) the Military Yearbook for Year X (except where otherwise noted) and (2) the 1812 Regulations were as follows (only one set of details is given if both sources are in agreement):

Regiment		Collar	Cuffs	Details
1		scarlet	scarlet	
2		green	scarlet	
3		scarlet	scarlet	
4		onquil	jonquil	
5		green	jonquil	yellow belting
6		jonquil	jonquil	
7		pink	pink	
8	(An VIII)	pink	pink	
	(1812)	green	pink	
9	(An VIII)	pink	green	
	(1812)	pink	pink	
10		crimson	crimson	
11	(An VIII)	crimson	crimson	
	(1812)	green	crimson	
12		crimson	crimson	
13		orange	orange	
14	(An VIII)	orange	orange	
	(1812)	green	orange	
15		orange	orange	
16		sky-blue	sky-blue	
17 & 18 [abolished]				
19	(An VIII)	aurore	aurore	aurore turban on shako
20	(An VIII)	aurore	aurore	
	(1812)	green	aurore	
21		aurore	aurore	
22		capucine	capucine	
23	(An VIII)	capucine	capucine	
	(1812)	green	capucine	
24	(An VIII)	yellow	scarlet	
	(1812)	capucine	capucine	
25		garance	garance	
26	(An XI & 1812)	green	garance	
27	(1812)	garance	garance	

Regiment		Collar	Cuffs	Details
28	(1812)	amaranth	amaranth	
29	(1812)	green	amaranth	
30	(1812)	amaranth	amaranth	
31	(1812)	buff	buff	

H. HUSSARS

The colourful uniforms of Napoleon's Hussars have inspired some in-depth studies of the dress of particular regiments (such as Commandant Bucquoy's work on the 1st Hussars), but there is no single general work that tackles the entire subject. The best modern summary is, once again, provided by the works of Rigo: 'Les Hussards, Troisième Epoque: Le Premier Empire et l' Epopée', in *Uniformes*, No. 34 (November–December 1976), pp. 28–33, and 'Les Aigles Triomphantes 1804-1812', in *Tradition*, No. 76 (December 1992), pp. 21–31.

The Martinet series includes the following four types of multi-subject Hussar print, all of which are generically reliable:

TYPE I – Mounted Hussar trooper in profile, pelisse worn off-shoulder, dated 1807. The spacing between the rows of braid on the dolman and the pelisse is unusually large.

TYPE II – Galloping Hussar aiming pistol. The way in which the figure in this Type of print is holding his pistol probably reflects the preferred technique for firing from horseback.

TYPE III – Galloping Hussar brandishing sabre. One state of this print shows a diamond-shaped shako plate, and in another the shako plate has been removed.

TYPE IV – Mounted Hussar Officer with leopard-skin saddle cloth. This print presents the archetypal full dress uniform of the Napoleonic period.

The uniform colours prescribed for the different Hussar regiments in (1) the Military Yearbook for Year X (except where otherwise noted) and (2) the 1812 Regulations were as follows (only one set of details is given if both sources are in agreement):

Regt	Dolman	Collar	Cuffs	Pelisse	Trousers	Braid & Buttons
1	sky-blue	sky-blue	red	sky-blue	sky-blue	white
2	brown	brown	sky-blue	brown	sky-blue	white
3	grey	grey	red	grey	grey	white
4	dark blue	dark blue	scarlet	scarlet	dark blue	yellow
5	sky-blue	sky-blue	white	white	sky-blue	yellow
6	red	red	red	dark blue	dark blue	yellow
7	green	scarlet	scarlet	green	green	yellow
8	green	scarlet	scarlet	green	green	white
9	scarlet	scarlet	scarlet	sky-blue	sky-blue	yellow
10	sky-blue	scarlet	scarlet	sky-blue	sky-blue	white
11	dark blue	scarlet	scarlet	dark blue	dark blue	yellow

For the uniform of the 12th Hussars of the Imperial era, see the text to Print No. 101/296.

I. LIGHT HORSE LANCERS

The basic Lancer uniform was formed by (1) a dragoon helmet modified by the addition of a rear visor and the substitution of a carabinier-style crest for the horse hair mane; (2) a dark green jacket with closed lapels, coloured facings and green shoulder- straps trimmed with the facing colour; and (3) dark green breeches worn with hussar boots, both of which had yellow trim.

The Martinet series includes the following two Types of print dealing with the six regiments of French Light Horse Lancers (as opposed to the three regiments of Lancers wearing Polish dress):

TYPE I – Mounted Lancer attacking with lowered lance. This print is the definitive primary source of information about the style and cut of the dress of the rank and file of French line lancer regiments. The jacket appears for the most part to follow the same pattern as an 1812-style infantry jacket (or 'Spencer'). There is, however, no sign of any ornament in the turnbacks of this figure, so the identification is incomplete. It is impossible to say whether the omission is intentional (because there were no ornaments) or inadvertent. An interesting point about the colours of the uniform is that the yellow braid and trim appears only on the trousers, boots and portmanteau.

TYPE II – Lancer officer on rearing horse. This print of a *Chevau-léger* officer is also the definitive primary source with respect to its chosen subject. The helmet clearly has a more stylised shape than that of the lancer in the Type I print. The officer seems to have an epaulette only on his left shoulder, which seems to identify him, at most, as a lieutenant or captain. The counter-epaulette which would be expected on the opposite shoulder for an infantry or Dragoon officer of the same rank is missing, a circumstance that suggests that the Line Lancers followed instead the style used by line Chasseur officers in this regard. The stripe along the outside seam of the breeches is unusual because it appears to be made up of three narrow stripes. The omission of an ornament in the corner of the saddle cloth is also noteworthy.

The facing colours prescribed for the different Lancer regiments in the 1812 Regulations were:

Regt	Lapels	Collar	Cuffs
1	scarlet	scarlet	scarlet
2	aurore	aurore	aurore
3	pink	pink	pink
4	crimson	crimson	crimson
5	sky-blue	sky-blue	sky-blue
6	madder red	madder red	madder red

J. LINE INFANTRY

Throughout most of Napoleon's reign, the appearance of his Line Infantry was, with the exception of the addition of the shako, little different from the appearance of the infantry of the French Revolutionary armies. As described in the Military Yearbook for Year X, the basic uniform consisted of:

> jacket *à la française* of national blue cloth, trimmed with red; white cloth lining; white lapels trimmed red; scarlet collar and cuffs trimmed white; white vest and breeches; yellow buttons (with the number of the demi-brigade [regiment]); white belts.[39]

The most obvious visual features of this outfit were the shako, the jacket cut away to expose the vest and the tall gaiters reaching above the knee. The 1812 Regulations changed both the jacket and the gaiters.

The Martinet series includes the following five Types of multi-subject Line Infantry prints, all of which are generically reliable:

TYPE I – Line Infantry Soldier with bearskin and shouldered musket, dated 1807. This print Type, and all other similar Types,

invariably have only two buttons on the cuff flap instead of the prescribed three.

TYPE II – Line Infantry Soldier with shako and shouldered musket, dated 1807.

TYPE III – Line Infantry Soldier with bicorne and shouldered musket, dated 1807.

TYPE IV – Line Infantry Grenadier resting hand on muzzle of musket. Although it does not constitute a true version of this print Type, the same figure pose is also used in Print No. 114/169.

TYPE V – Line Infantry Officer holding drawn sword.

K. LIGHT INFANTRY

The basic Light Infantry uniform is described in detail in the *État Militaire* for Year X:

> Uniform – Jacket [*habit-veste*] of dark blue cloth, with 'Hungarian-style', triangular blue lapels piped with white; blue cuffs piped white; red collar, blue vest, blue trousers; half-gaiters, hat or shako with small tuft [*houpette*]; button bearing number of the unit.[40]

The most distinctive aspect of this uniform was the predominance of the colour blue, but it also differed from that of the Line Infantry in the shape of the lapels and in the fact that the tails of the jacket were cut significantly shorter (in theory, at least, to allow freer movement by the wearer). Light Infantry soldiers also wore a different pattern of gaiter cut to just below the knee and usually decorated with coloured trim and a tassel around its upper edge.

The Martinet series includes the following three different Types of multi-subject Light Infantry prints, all of which are generically reliable:

TYPE I – Light Infantry Soldier with bearskin and shouldered musket, dated 1807.

Type II – Light Infantry Soldier with shako and shouldered musket, dated 1807.

Type III – Light Infantry Officer holding drawn sword.

L. ARTILLERY

Napoleon's artillery was dressed predominantly in blue with red cuffs and trim. For most of the period Foot Artillerymen wore the same style of uniform as Line Infantrymen, and Horse Artillerymen wore the same style of uniform as either the Hussars (without the pelisse) or the Chasseurs. The 1812 Regulations assigned the same style uniform to both Horse and Foot Artillery of the Line, but distinctions persisted.

M. AUXILIARY TROOPS

In his unceasing search for soldiers to fill the ranks of his vast military machine, Napoleon created a significant number of auxiliary military formations which were lumped under the general heading of 'Troupes Hors Ligne' or 'Troops Outside the Line [of Battle]'. As the title indicates, these units were typically intended to perform only garrison, policing or other paramilitary functions, but in practice they often ended up on active service.

1. Paris Municipal Guard

The decree creating the Paris Guard is very specific on the subject of its uniforms:

XXV. The form of the head-dress, coat and shoes of the two regiments of infantry of the Municipal Guard of Paris will be the same as that established for line infantry.

The first regiment will have a green coat lined with white, white vest and trousers, black gaiters and red collar, cuffs and lapels.

The second regiment will have a red coat, white vest and trousers, green cuffs, collar and lapels and black gaiters.

The red uniform of the Second Regiment was sufficiently unique that they were dubbed the 'crayfish' by the rest of the Grande Armée.[41] It is somewhat remarkable that this unusual uniform was not included in the extensive run of prints which Martinet devoted, naturally enough, to his local municipal guard.

The 1812 Regulations confirm that the dress of the Paris Guard ultimately changed to a white uniform with green collar cuffs and lapels. They also include the iron-grey and red colours of the Dragoons of the Paris Guard.

Since the uniforms for the Paris Guard were the same style as the uniforms for Line Infantry, they were produced for the series using the multi-subject prints for the Line Infantry.

2. Gendarmes

Apart from the Paris Guard, the Foot Gendarmes are the only other auxiliary unit mentioned in the 1812 Regulations, which confirm the traditional blue and red colour scheme of this force. There were two types of Mounted Gendarmes, each having its own style of uniform. The majority of them had a uniform almost identical with that of the Foot Gendarmes. The Light Horse Gendarmes, which were raised specifically for anti-guerrilla service in Spain, had a uniform modelled on the undress uniform of the Mounted Chasseurs of the Guard and were armed with lances.[42]

3. State Schools

Although none is reproduced in this book, there are several prints of state school students in the series, presumably because most of the schools dressed their students in military uniforms. They were all produced by means of multi-subject prints.

N. FOREIGN TROOPS

The only foreign troops mentioned explicitly in the 1812 Regulations were the Polish Line

Lancers and the four Swiss infantry regiments.

1. Polish Light Horse Lancers

These were the three regiments of *Chevau-Legere Lancers* which were not created from Dragoon regiments. The basic uniform consisted of (1) a Polish shako (*czapska*); (2) a dark blue Polish-style jacket (*kurtka*) with coloured facings and blue shoulder-straps trimmed with the facing colour; (3) dark blue, tight-fitting trousers. All regiments wore a wide, blue, decorative waistbelt with three horizontal white stripes. The facing colours specified in the 1812 Regulations were:

Regiment	Lapels	Collar	Cuffs
7	yellow	yellow	yellow
8	yellow	blue	blue
9	chamois	chamois	chamois

2. Swiss Infantry

The basic uniform consisted of a red coat and white trousers. The cut of the uniform, headdress, elite company distinctions and equipment were all the same as for French Line Infantry. The facing colours for the four regiments in the 1812 Regulations were:

Regiment	Lapels	Collar	Cuffs	Cuff Flap	Pocket
1	yellow	yellow	yellow	red	horizontal
2	dark blue	dark blue	dark blue	dark blue	horizontal
3	black	black	black	white	horizontal
4	sky-blue	sky-blue	sky-blue	sky-blue	horizontal

3. Other Foreign Regiments

Although they are not dealt with in the 1812 Regulations, the French Army itself (as opposed to its allied contingents) included four regiments which were specifically intended to be recruited from citizens of foreign countries. Two of these mercenary units, the Isembourg Regiment and the 3rd Foreign Regiment (formerly the Irish Legion), are covered in the series by multi-subject Light Infantry prints. The other two, the Tour d'Auvergne Regiment and the Prussian Regiment, are not. The status of the Portuguese Legion was different in theory, because for a long time Napoleon clung to the possibility that it would represent a contingent from one of his satellite kingdoms, but after the failure of the 1810–11 attempt to re-conquer Portugal, it was not different in practice.

INTRODUCTION

NOTES

1 One of the few works to recognise the value of Martinet's work is Philip J. Haythornthwaite's article 'Interpreting Napoleonic Prints' in *Military Illustrated* No. 6 (April/May 1987), pp 36–43.

2 All the biographical details concerning Martinet in this work are taken from an article by Louis Hautecoeur entitled 'Une Famille de Graveurs et d'Editeurs Parisiens: Les Martinets et les Hautecoeurs (XVIII et XIX Siècles) (hereinafter referred to as 'Hautecoeur'), in *Paris et Ile-de-France: Mémoires*, vols. 18–19 (1967–8), pp. 205–340. This journal is the house publication of the Fédération des Sociétés Historiques et Archéologiques de Paris et de l'Ile-de-France.

3 Martinet's plate of the Greater Frigate Bird is reproduced in Maureen Lambourne, *The Art of Bird Illustration* (Secaucus, New Jersey, 1990), p. 100.

4 Most of the technical information in this volume about prints and print-making comes from Bamber Gascoigne's *How to Identify Prints* (London, 1986) (hereinafter referred to as 'Gascoigne'), a work which is extremely useful in study of old military prints.

5 *Le Publiciste*, issue of 24 *Vendémiaire* Year IX (15 October 1800), quoted in Hautecoeur, p. 274.

6 Hautecoeur, p. 289.

7 Hautecoeur, p. 284, quoting Joseph-Etienne de (self-styled) Jouy, *L'Hermite de la Chaussée d'Antin* (5 vols., Paris 1813), vol. 1, p. 177.

8 This lithograph is reproduced as Illustration No. III in Hautecoeur following p. 248 and is discussed in some detail on pp. 282–3.

9 This expansion is evidenced by information on the prints themselves. Although most of the prints dated 1808 bear the address of Rue du Coq No. 15 (see, e.g., Print No. 52), two of them (Print Nos. 59 and 60) have a return address of 'Rue du Coq No. **13 et** 15' (author's emphasis).

10 A list of these prints is provided in *Costumes Militaires – Catalogue des Principales Suites de Costumes Militaires Français Parues tant en France qu'à l'Etranger depuis le Règne de Louis XV jusqu'à nos Jours et des Suites de Costumes Militaires Etrangers Parues en France* (Paris, 1900) by '*Un Membre de la Sabretache*' (Glasser) (hereinafter referred to as 'Glasser'), pp. 30–2. Glasser makes the same editorial point that Basset's prints are 'imitations' of, and 'notably inferior to', similar prints by Martinet.

11 The prints in this edition are listed in Glasser, pp. 313–14. A typical transformation for this series is the alteration of an Officer of the Imperial Guard Grenadiers to represent a Grenadier Officer of one of the Departmental Legions created by the Bourbons.

12 The prints are listed in Glasser, pp. 457–9.

13 In this book the term 'Type' is used to differentiate the multi-subject prints used by Martinet to illustrate a particular type of soldier from the *Grande Armée*. An inventory of all the Types of prints in the series is provided in Section IV below.

14 A two-part numerical designation has been used for all Martinet print references in the text: the number before the oblique stroke is that assigned to the print in the sequence of reproductions in this book, the second number being that assigned to the print by Martinet in the *Troupes Françaises* series. So the description 'Print No. 135/1' indicates that the 135th print reproduced in this book is Print No. 1 from the series.

15 Hautecoeur, pp. 287–8.

16 Emmanuel Bénézit (ed.), *Dictionnaire Critique et Documentaire des Peintres, Sculpteurs, Dessinateurs et Graveurs* (Paris, numerous edns.).

17 See, e.g., the attribution in the 'Notes on Artists' in Henri Lachouque and Anne S. K. Brown, *The Anatomy of Glory* (Providence, RI, 1962), p. 527.

18 Hautecoeur, pp. 249, 288.

19 Hautecoeur, p. 288.

20 Gascoigne, Section 48a. (This work does not have page numbers.)

21 The introduction to the catalogue of Martinet's prints in Glasser mentions the existence of larger size prints ('*Edition en grand papier*') having dimensions of 22cm by 29.6cm, but the author has not actually seen any examples of prints from this de-luxe edition. Glasser, p. 320.

22 'Deposited at the Bibliothèque Impériale', which was necessary under French law of the time to establish ownership in the copyright of a printed work.

23 The one piece of additional evidence which would definitely confirm this hypothesis would be the existence of significant numbers of dated prints without series numbers, but the author has never seen an example of such a print.

24 René Colas, *Bibliographie générale du costume et de la mode* ... (2 vols., Paris, 1933), vol. 2, p. 733.

25 A total of three Types of multi-subject prints are used in the *Troupes Françaises* series to illustrate Chasseur uniforms. A list of them is provided in Section IV below.

26 Captain Sauzey, in his famous work *Iconographie du Costume Militaire de la Révolution et de l'Empire* (Paris, 1901), does inexplicably include (at p. 286) a mention of a Print No. 309 depicting a soldier of the 3rd Swiss Regiment, but otherwise all the prints he cites are within the 1–296 range.

27 This practice led to a mistake in respect of at least one print. The series includes a second state of Print No. 144/17 (Departmental Guard of Paris in 1808) showing a soldier of that unit in a sky-blue 1812-style jacket with closed lapels. However, since the colour of the uniform of that unit was changed to white (see Print No. 145/126), it is extremely unlikely that the Departmental Guard ever issued a second version of the original sky-blue uniform.

28 One of these, the original painting for the first state of print of the Dutch Grenadiers of the Guard (Print No. 34/214.1), has been reproduced in Pierre de Hugo and Bertrand Malvaux, 'Les Bonnets à Poils de la Garde Impériale 1804–1805', in *Tradition* No. 93 (October, 1994), pp. 19–20, at 19.

29 There is even one documented case of a soldier in one of the Young Guard squadrons of the 1st Scout Lancers of the Imperial Guard who compensated for the fact that Martinet did not publish a print of that unit to 'make' one himself by re-colouring an existing print of the 3rd Chasseurs. Jean and Raoul Brunon, *Les Eclaireurs de la Garde Impériale 1813–1814* (Marseilles n.d.), cover illustration and p. 22.

30 It might be argued that the 1812 Regulations (as defined in the next section) and the related paintings by Carle Vernet illustrating the uniforms decreed therein might together have constituted such a source, but since they were not in existence prior to 1812, they could not have influenced Martinet's earlier work.

31 Gille Boué, '*Le Bataillon des Déserteurs Français Rentrés 1802–1814*', in *Uniformes* No. 112 (March, 1988), pp. 5–10.

32 The decrees were published in *Journal Militaire*, Pt. 1, 1812, pp. 5–17, 42–75.

33 *Journal Militaire*, Pt. 1, 1806, p. 65.

34 *Journal Militaire*, Pt. 1, 1806, pp. 176–7; Pt. 2, pp. 14–15.

35 This information is most accessible through a compilation by Gustave Marchal entitled *Les Uniformes de l'Armée Française sous Le Consulat* (Paris, 1901), which presents the uniform information from the Military Yearbooks for Years VIII, X and XI (there does not appear to have been a Yearbook for Year IX). Although there were Yearbooks for Years XII and XIII, they do not contain any uniform details. The Military Yearbook series was cancelled by Napoleon thereafter because of his reasonable concern that it made too much sensitive information available to France's enemies.

36 *Journal Militaire* for Year X, Pt. 1, pp. 173–9.

37 See this author's *Napoleon's Soldiers: The Grande Armée of 1807 as Depicted in the Paintings of the Otto Manuscript* (London, 1994).

38 See, e.g., the photographs of dolmans of the 11th, 13th and 16th Chasseurs in Rigo, I, pp. 30–6.

39 Quoted in Marchal, *Les Uniformes*, p. 9.

40 Quoted in Marchal, *Les Uniformes*, p. 10.

41 L. C. Coqueugniot, *Histoire de la Légion du Nord – Mémoire de L. C. Coqueugniot, Major* (Beauchevain, Belgium, 1992), p. 98. This work is a reprint by Bernard Coppens of a memoir which originally appeared in the *Nouvelle Revue Rétrospective* in 1898.

42 A comprehensive summary of the organisation and dress of Napoleon's Gendarmes can be found in the first section of Emmanuel Martin's *La Gendarmerie Française en Espagne et en Portugal (Campagnes de 1807 à 1814)*, Paris, 1898.

PRINT REPRODUCTIONS

PRINT REPRODUCTIONS

This Section contains reproductions of 162 engravings from the *Troupes Françaises* series. Commentaries for these reproductions can be found in Section II. The prints reproduced have been chosen to provide a representative selection of the full complement of prints in the series while eliminating excessive reproduction of multi-subject prints. The prints have been grouped into the same general subject categories as the uniform information in Section IV above in order to facilitate cross-references. This is the reason why the sequence of prints in this book is different from the sequence of prints in the series itself. (Please note that the commentaries and Appendixes A and B provide both numerical designations for each print.)

Pl. 180.

Troupes Françaises.

A Paris chez Martinet, Libraire, rue du Coq N.° 13 et 15.

1/180.1

Maréchal de l'Empire.

A Paris, chez Martinet, Libraire, rue du Coq, N.° 13 et 15.

Pl. 197

Troupes Françaises.

Général de Brigade

A Paris, chez Martinet, Libraire, rue du Coq n.º 13 et 15.

Pl. 272   *Troupes Françaises.*

A Paris chez Martinet Libraire rue du Coq N.º 13 et 15.

Aide de Camp.
de Mestre de Camp.

Capitaine adjoint aux Etat major des Armées.

A Paris chez Martinet, Libraire, rue du Coq. N:13 et 15.

Pl. 192

Troupes Françaises

Commissaire des guerres

A Paris chez Martinet, Libraire, rue du Coq, N.º 13 et 15.

Pl. 210.

Troupes Françaises.

A Paris chez Martinet, Libraire, rue du Coq, N°. 13 et 15.

Sous-Inspecteur aux revues.

Chirurgien de 1ere Classe.

A Paris, chez Martinet, Libraire, rue du Coq, N.º 13 et 15.

A Paris chez Martinet, Libraire, rue du Coq N°15.

Malœuvre

GARDE IMPÉRIALE
Grenadier à Cheval

Pl. 184

Troupes Françaises.

A Paris chez Martinet, Libraire, rue du Coq N.º 13 et 15.

GARDE IMPÉRIALE
Officier des Grenadiers à Cheval

Troupes Françaises

GARDE IMPÉRIALE
Dragon

Pl. 225

Troupes Françaises.

A.Paris, chez Martinet, Libraire, rue du Coq, N° 13 et 15.

Dragons de la Garde Impériale.
Officier.

Pl. 230

Troupes Françaises

A Paris chez Martinet, Libraire, rue du Coq R.° 13 et 15.

DRAGONS DE LA GARDE IMPÉRIALE.

Trompettes,
Grand et petit uniforme.

Dragon de la R. en p.te tenue.

A Paris chez Martinet, Libraire, rue du Coq H. 13 et 15.

14/259.1

GARDE IMPERIALE

Gendarme d'Elite

A Paris, chez Martinet, Libraire, rue du Coq N.º 15.

A Paris, chez Martinet, Libraire, rue du Coq, N°. 13 et 15.

GARDE IMPÉRIALE
Officier des Gendarmes d'Élite

A Paris chez Martinet Libraire rue du Coq N.º 15

GARDE IMPÉRIALE.

Chasseurs à Cheval

Pl. 14 185 *Troupes Françaises.*

A Paris chez Martinet, libraire, rue du Coq N.° 13 et 15.

GARDE IMPÉRIALE

Chasseur à cheval en petit uniforme.

A Paris, chez Martinet, Libraire, rue du Coq, N.º 13 et 15.

GARDE IMPÉRIALE
Officier des Guides (Petit Uniforme.)

A Paris chez Martinet, libraire, rue du Coq, N.º 13 et 15.

Officier des Chasseurs à cheval de la Garde.

A Paris, chez Martinet, Libraire, rue du Coq, N.º 13 et 15.

Trompette des Chasseurs de la Garde.

Pl. 158

Troupes Françaises

A Paris chez Martinet, Libraire rue du Coq R. 13 et 15

GARDE IMPÉRIALE

Mamduck

Chevau-leger polonois, de la G.de

A Paris chez Martinet, Libraire, rue du Coq N.º 13 et 15

Pl. 265.　　　　　　　　　　　　　　　　　　Troupes Françaises.

Lancier de la Garde 1.ᵉʳ Reg.ᵗ

Paris chez Martinet, Libraire, rue du Coq. N.ᵒ 13 et 15.

Pl. 206

Troupes Françaises.

A Paris chez Martinet, Libraire, rue du Coq N.° 15 et 13.

GARDE IMPÉRIALE,

Timbalier des Lanciers Polonois.

Pl. 217

Troupes Françaises.

A Paris chez Martinet, Libraire, rue du Coq, N.º 13 et 15.

Officier des Lanciers Polonois,
de la Garde
en 1813.

Pl. 251   Troupes Françaises

A Paris chez Martinet, Libraire, rue du Coq. N.° 13 et 15

GARDE IMPÉRIALE
Lancier 2.e Rég.t

Pl. 252

A Paris chez Martinet, Libraire, rue du Coq, N.º 13 et 15.

Officier des Lanciers de la Garde,
2.ᵉ Rég.ᵗ

A Paris, chez Martinet, Libraire, rue du Coq, N° 13 et 15.

GARDE D'HONNEUR,
3. *Régiment.*

29/292.2

A Paris, chez Martinet, Libraire, rue du Coq N.º15

GARDE IMPÉRIALE

Grenadiers

Pl. 117.

Troupes Françaises

A Paris chez Martinet, Libraire, rue du Coq N°. 13 et 15

Grenadier de la Garde Impériale
et
M.^{de} d'Eau-de-vie suivant l'Armée.

A Paris, chez Martinet, Libraire, rue du Coq, N.º 13 et 15.

GARDE IMPÉRIALE

Officier des Grenadiers à pied.

Pl. 120.

Troupes Françaises.

GARDE IMPÉRIALE,
Sapeur des Grenadiers

GARDE IMPÉRIALE

Grenadier 3.ᵉ Régiment

A Paris, chez Martinet, Libraire, rue du Coq, N.ᵒ 13 et 15.

34/214.1

A Paris chez Martinet, Libraire, rue du Coq N.º 13 et 15.

GARDE IMPÉRIALE

Officier des Grenadiers 3 *Régiment*

GARDE IMPÉRIALE
Chasseurs.

A Paris, chez Martinet, Libraire, rue du Coq N° 15

36/54

Pl 107.

Troupes Françaises

Paris, chez Martinet, Libraire rue du Coq, N.° 13 et 15.

Officiers de Chasseurs
de la Garde Impériale.

Troupes Francaises

GARDE IMPÉRIALE
Fusilier.

A Paris chez Martinet, Libraire, rue du Coq N.º 15

Pl. 172.

Troupes Françaises

GARDE IMPÉRIALE

Fusillier-Grenadier

Pl. 118

Troupes Françaises

GARDE IMPÉRIALE

Tirailleurs

Pl. 118

Troupes Françaises

A Paris chez Martinet, Libraire, rue du Coq N.° 13 et 15

GARDE IMPÉRIALE

Tirailleurs

Voltigeurs.

41/118.1

Pl. 121

A Paris chez Martinet, Libraire, rue du Coq N° 13 et 15.

GARDE IMPÉRIALE

Tirailleurs

Grenadiers - Conscrits.

Pl. 176.

Troupes Françaises.

A Paris chez Martinet, Libraire, rue du Coq Nº 13 et 15

GARDE IMPÉRIALE
Tambour - major

GARDE IMPÉRIALE

Musicien des Grenadiers à pied.

A Paris, chez Martinet, Libraire, rue du Coq, N.º 13 et 15.

A Paris chez Martinet, Libraire, rue du Coq, N.º 13 et 15.

GARDE IMPÉRIALE

Flanqueur

Pl. 213.

Troupes Françaises.

Canonier à pied de la G.de

A Paris chez Martinet, Libraire, rue du Coq N.3 et 15.

Pl. 198

Troupes Françaises.

Canonier à cheval, de la Garde.

A Paris chez Martinet, Libraire, rue du Coq N.º 13 et 15.

Pl. 36

Troupes Françaises.

A Paris chez Martinet, Libraire, rue du Coq N.º 13 et 15.

Canonier à Cheval en p.te tenue.

48/36.1

A Paris, chez Martinet, Libraire, rue du Coq. N.º 13 et 15.

GARDE IMPÉRIALE

Officier d'Artillerie à cheval.

A Paris chez Martinet, Libraire, rue du Coq N.º 13 et 15.

Ex - Garde,
Train, en 1813.

Pl. 101

Troupes Françaises

GARDE IMPÉRIALE

Train

A Paris chez Martinet, Libraire, rue du Coq N.° 13 et 15.

51/101

GARDE IMPÉRIALE
Sapeur du Génie.
A Paris, chez Martinet, Libraire, rue du Coq, N.º 13 et 15.

A Paris chez Martinet Libraire, rue du Coq N.º 13 et 15.
GARDE IMPÉRIALE
Officier des Sapeurs du Génie.

A Paris chez Martinet Libraire rue du Coq N.° 15

GARDE IMPÉRIALE.
Marin

Pl. 104

Troupes Françaises

Carabinier à cheval
2.e Régiment
en 1807

A Paris chez Martinet Libraire, rue du Coq R.^o 13 et 15

A Paris, chez Martinet, Libraire, rue du Coq, N° 13 et 15.

Carabinier à Cheval
Régiment.

A Paris, chez Martinet, Libraire, rue du Coq. No 3 et 15

Officier de Carabinier à Cheval.

Pl. 216

Troupes Françaises.

A Paris chez Martinet, Libraire, rue du Coq N.º 13 et 15

Trompette de Cuirassiers.
1.ᵉ Regiment.

Dep. a la Bib. Imp.   A Paris chez Martinet, Libraire, rue du Coq N.º 15.

Cuirassiers

H.ᵗ Rey

Pl. 204

Troupes Françaises.

Trompette de Cuirassiers.
4. *Regiment.*

Pl. 86

Troupes Françaises.

A Paris, chez Martinet, Libraire, rue du Coq N.º 13 et 15.

Cuirassiers

5.ᵉ Régiment.

Dep. à la Bib. Imp.

A Paris chez Martinet, Libraire, rue du Coq N° 15.

Cuirassiers
7.ᵉ Régt.

Pl. 209

Troupes Françaises

A.Paris chez Martinet, libraire rue du Coq. Nº13 et 15

CUIRASSIERS

Officier Superieur

7 Regiment

Pl. 240

Troupes Françaises.

Trompette de Cuirassiers.
7⁵ Regiment.

A Paris chez Martinet, Libraire, rue du Coq N⁰ 13 et 15

64/240

Pl. 153.

Troupes Françaises.

A Paris, chez Martinet, libraire, rue du Coq N.º 13 et 15.

Cuirassiers.

13. *Régiment.*

DRAGONS.

Brigadier 4.e Régiment. Départ du Cantonnement.

A Paris chez Martinet. Libraire rue du Coq N.° 13 et 15.

Pl. 163.

Troupes Françaises

A Paris chez Martinet, Libraire, rue du Coq N.° 13 et 15

Officier de Dragon
6.° Régiment

Pl. 36

Troupes Françaises

CAVALERIE LÉGERE, *Dragon,*
Compagnie d'Elite,
7.ᵉ *Régiment.*

A Paris chez Martinet, Libraire, rue du Coq Nᵒ. 13 et 15.

68/36.2

A Paris chez Martinet, Libraire, rue du Coq, N.° 13 et 15.

Officier de Dragons.

14.° Rég.t — Colonel.

Pl. 85

Troupes Françaises

CAVALERIE LEGERE, *Dragon*
17.ᵉ *Régiment*

Pl. 166

Troupes Françaises

A Paris chez Martinet, Libraire, rue du Coq St. 13 et 15

Officier de Dragon
19 Régiment

71/166.1

A Paris chez Martinet, Libraire rue du Coq N.º 15   Dep. à la Bib.

CAVALERIE LÉGÈRE, *Dragon*
22. *Régiment*

A Paris chez Martinet, Libraire rue du Coq N.º 15   Dep. à la Bib.

CAVALERIE LÉGERE, *Dragon*
25. *Régiment.*

Pl. 183

Troupes Françaises

CAVALERIE LÉGÈRE, Dragon,
Compagnie d'Élite,
2e. Régiment.
en 1810

Pl. 37

Troupes Françaises

A Paris chez Martinet Libraire, rue du Coq N° 13 et 15

CAVALERIE LÉGERE, *Dragon*
29. *Régiment*

DRAGONS.
Gilet et pantalon d'écurie. Pansement du matin.
A Paris chez Martinet, Libraire, rue du Coq, N.° 13 et 15.

Pl. 189

Troupes Françaises.

Officier de Chasseurs à Cheval
2.   Régiment
Compagnie d'Elite

A Paris chez Martinet, Libraire, rue du Coq N.º 13 et 15

77/189.1

Pl. 73 bis   *Troupes Françaises*

A.Paris chez Martinet, Libraire, rue du Coq N.º 13 et 15.

Chasseurs à cheval
3.ᵉ Régiment
Compagnie d'Elite

Dép. à la Bib. Imp.

A Paris chez Martinet, Libraire, rue du Coq N°.15

Chasseurs à cheval
5.ᵉ Régiment.

Pl. 481

Troupes Françaises.

A Paris chez Martinet, Libraire, rue du Coq Nᵒˢ 13 et 15.

Officier de Chasseurs à Cheval
6.ᵉ Régiment.

Pl. 43.

Troupes Françaises

Chasseurs à cheval

7. *Régiment*

A Paris chez Martinet, Libraire, rue du Coq N.º 13 et 15

81/43.1

Troupes Françaises

Dép. à la Bib. Imp.

A Paris chez Martinet, Libraire, rue du Coq N.° 15

Chasseurs à cheval

11.e Regiment

82/95

Chasseurs à cheval
16.º Regiment

Pl. 90

A Paris chez Martinet, Libraire, rue du Coq N° 15 et 13

Chasseurs à cheval
23.ᵉ Régiment

Pl. 102.

Troupes Françaises

A Paris chez Martinet, Libraire, rue du Coq N.º 13 et 15

Chasseurs à cheval
27. Régiment

Dep. à la Bib. Imp.

A Paris chez Martinet, Libraire rue du Coq N.º 15.

Hussard

1. Régiment

Pl. 128.

Troupes Françaises

A Paris chez Marlinet, Libraire, rue du Coq N° 13 et 15.

Officier d'Hussard
1. Régiment

Troupes Françaises

Dép. à la Bib. Imp.

A Paris chez Martinet, Libraire rue du Coq N.º 15

Hussard

2.ᵉ *Régiment.*

Pl. 8 — *Troupes Françaises*

A Paris chez Martinet, Libraire, rue du Coq N.º 13 et 15

Hussard
3.ᵉ Regiment

89/8.2

Pl 140.

Troupes Françaises

A Paris chez Martinet, Libraire, rue du Coq N.° 13 et 15.

Officier d'Hussard
3.º Régiment

Dep. à la Bib. Imp.

A Paris chez Martinet, Libraire rue du Coq N.º 15.

Hussard
A.ᵉ *Régiment*

91/10

Pl. 11

Troupes Françaises

A Paris chez Martinet, Libraire, rue du Coq N.º 13 et 15

Hussard
5.ᵉ Regiment

92/11.1

Pl 134

Troupes Françaises

A Paris chez Martinet, Libraire, rue du Coq N° 13 et 15.

Officier d'Hussard
5. *Régiment.*

Dép. à la Bib. Imp.

A Paris chez Martinet, libraire rue du Coq Nº 15

Hussard
6ᵉ Régiment.

Dép. à la Bib. Imp.

À Paris chez Martinet, Libraire rue du Coq N.° 15.

Hussard
7. Régiment.

Pl. 31

Troupes Françaises

A Paris chez Martinet, Libraire, rue du Coq n°. 15 et 16.

Hufsard
8.ᵉ Régiment
en 1813

Dép. à la Bib. Imp.

A Paris chez Martinet, Libraire rue du Coq N.° 15.

Hussard
Régiment
de 1806 à 1814.

Pl. 33.

Troupes Françaises

A Paris chez Martinet, Libraire, rue du Coq N.º 15 et 15

Hussard
10.º *Régiment*

Pl. 122.

Troupes Françaises

A Paris chez Martinet, Libraire, rue du Coq N.º 13 et 15.

Officier d'Hussard
10 Régiment

Hussard

11. Regiment

Hussard
12.ᵉ *Regiment*

A Paris, chez Martinet, Libraire, rue du Coq, N.º 13 et 15.

Chevau-légers Français.
1. Régiment.

A Paris, chez Martinet Libraire, rue du Coq N.º 13 et 15.

Officier des Chevau-legers Français.
1 *Régiment*

A Paris, chez Martinet, Libraire, rue du Coq, N.º 13 et 15.

Chevau-légers Français.
2.ᵉ Régiment

A Paris chez Martinet Libraire, rue du Coq N.º 13 et 15.

Officier des Chevau-legers Français.
4. Régiment

105/260.1

A Paris chez Martinet Libraire, rue du Coq N.º 13 et 15.

Officier des Chevau-legers Français.
5.ᵉ Régiment.

A Paris chez Martinet Libraire, rue du Coq N.º 15.   Dep. à la Bib. Imp.

INFANTERIE DE LIGNE
15. Régiment

Voltigeur

A Paris chez Martinet Libraire rue du Coq N.º 15.

Dep. à la Bib. Imp.

INFANTERIE DE LIGNE, *Chasseur*

Regiment

en 1807

108/34.1

A Paris chez Martinet, Libraire, rue du Coq N.º 13.   Dép. à la Bib. Imp.

INFANTERIE DE LIGNE, *Grenadier*
15.ᵉ *Régiment*

Pl. 133.

Troupes Françaises

INFANTERIE DE LIGNE

19 Régiment

A Paris chez Martinet, Libraire, rue du Coq N.° 15.   Dép. à la Bib. Imp.

INFANTERIE DE LIGNE, *Grenadier*
32. *Régiment*
en 1807.

A Paris chez Martinet Libraire, rue du Coq N.º 15.   Dép. à la Bib. Imp.

INFANTERIE DE LIGNE
32. Regiment

A Paris chez Martinet, Libraire, rue du Coq N.º 15.

Dép. à la Bib. Imp.

INFANTERIE DE LIGNE, *Grenadier*
58 Régiment

Pl. 169

Troupes Françaises

A Paris chez Martinet, Libraire rue du Coq N.º 13 et 15.

INFANTERIE DE LIGNE
100.º Régiment.

A Paris chez Martinet Libraire rue du Coq N° 15.

Dép. à la Bib. Imp.

INFANTERIE DE LIGNE, *Chasseur*
122. Regiment
1809.

115/3.1

Pl. 5

Troupes Françaises

A Paris chez Martinet Libraire rue du Coq N°s 13 et 15

INFANTERIE DE LIGNE

Régiment

Grenadier

INFANTERIE DE LIGNE
Fourier

A Paris chez Martinet Libraire, rue du Coq, N°.13 et 15.

117/16.1

Pl. 111.

Troupes Françaises.

INFANTERIE DE LIGNE
Sergent-major
plantant son Aigle sur une Redoute enlevée de vive force

118/111

A Paris chez Martinet, Libraire, rue du Coq N.º 13 et 15

INFANTERIE DE LIGNE
Tambour Major.

Pl. 161

Troupes Françaises

A Paris chez Martinet, Libraire rue du Coq N° 13 et 15

INFANTERIE DE LIGNE

Tambour battant la Diane

Pl. 201

Troupes Françaises.

Officier d'Infanterie de Ligne.

A Paris chez Martinet Libraire, rue du Coq N.º 13 et 15.

121/201

Pl. 224

Troupes Françaises.

A Paris chez Martinet, Libraire rue du Coq N.º 13 et 15.

INFANTERIE DE LIGNE EN CAMPAGNE.

Sentinelle

INFANTERIE DE LIGNE
Caporal

A Paris, chez Martinet, Libraire, rue du Coq, N.º 13 et 15.

SCÈNE MILITAIRE.

A Paris, chez Martinet, Libraire, rue du Coq, N.º 13 et 15.

INFANTERIE DE LIGNE.
Sergent.

A Paris chez Martinet, Libraire, rue du Coq. N.º 13 et 15.

125/249.1

INFANTERIE DE LIGNE

Maître d'Armes.

A Paris chez Martinet, Libraire, rue du Coq H.º 13 et 15

Infanterie de ligne en 1813.

127/280.1

A.Paris, chez Martinet, rue du Coq N.º 15.　　　Dep. à la Bib. Imp.

INFANTERIE LÉGERE. *Chasseur*
2.ᵉ Régiment
Voltigeur.

A Paris, chez Martinet, rue du Coq N° 15.   Dep. à la Bib. Imp.

INFANTERIE LÉGERE. *Chasseur*

Régiment

Voltigeur *De 1806 à 1814.*

129/23.1

A Paris chez Martinet, Libraire, rue du Coq N.º 15.

Dep. a la Bib. Imp.

INFANTERIE LÉGERE, *Carabinier*

Régiment

130/24.2

INFANTERIE LÉGERE
Caporal

A Paris chez Martinet Libraire rue du Coq, N.º 13 et 15.

A Paris, chez Martinet, Libraire, rue du Coq, N.° 13 et 15.

INFANTERIE LÉGERE.

Carabinier.

A.Paris chez Martinet, Libraire, rue du Coq N.° 13 et 15

CANONNIER.

133/59

Pl. 60

CANONNIER A CHEVAL

A Paris chez Martinet, Libraire, rue du Coq N.º 13 et 15.

134/60.1

A. Paris chez Martinet, Libraire, rue du Coq R.º 15.   *Dép. à la Bib. Imp.*

INFANTERIE DE LIGNE, *Grenadier*

1.ᵉ Régiment

Garde de Paris

A Paris chez Martinet, Libraire, rue du Coq N° 15.

Dep. à la Bib. Imp.

INFANTERIE DE LIGNE, *Grenadier*

1^r *Régiment*
Garde de Paris.

136/1.1

A Paris chez Martinet Libraire, rue du Coq N.º 15.   Dep. à la Bib. Imp.

INFANTERIE DE LIGNE
1.ᵉʳ Régiment
Garde de Paris

Troupes Françaises

(1807)

A Paris chez Martinet Libraire rue du Coq N.º 15.

Dép. à la Bib. Imp.

INFANTERIE DE LIGNE, *Chasseur*

1. *Regiment*

Garde de Paris

A Paris chez Martinet, Libraire, rue du Coq N.º 15.   Dép. à la Bib. Imp.

INFANTERIE DE LIGNE, *Grenadier - Chasseur Voltigeur, 1. Régiment Garde de Paris. en 1810.*

139/170

Pl. 243.

Troupes Françaises.

Officier d'Infanterie de Ligne
1. Rég. Garde de Paris.
A Paris chez Martinet Libraire, rue du Coq N.° 13 et 15.

A Paris chez Martinet Libraire rue du Coq N.° 15.   Dép. à la Bib. Imp.

INFANTERIE DE LIGNE, *Chasseur*
2.ᵉ Regiment
Garde de Paris

A Paris chez Martinet, Libraire, rue du Coq N.º 15. Dep. à la Bib. Imp.

INFANTERIE DE LIGNE, *Carabinier*
du 2.e Régiment de la
Garde de Paris.

Pl. 106 *Troupes Françaises*

CAVALERIE LÉGÈRE., *Dragon*
Garde de Paris

A Paris chez Martinet, Libraire rue du Coq N.º 15.   Dép. à la Bib. Imp.

Garde départementale de Paris
en 1808.

Pl. 126

Troupes Françaises

A Paris chez Martinet Libraire rue du Coq N.° 13 et 15

INFANTERIE DE LIGNE

1. Régiment

Garde départementale, 1.re Comp.ie

A Paris chez Martinet, Libraire rue du Coq N.º 15.   Dép. à la Bib. Imp.

Garde National.

Bataillon de Chasseurs
de Flessingue.

147/127.1

A Paris chez Martinet Libraire, rue du Coq N.° 15.   Dep. à la Bib. Imp.

INFANTERIE DE LIGNE

Regiment

1. *Bataillon colonial*

A Paris chez Martinet Libraire rue du Coq N.° 15.   Dep. à la Bib. Imp.

INFANTERIE DE LIGNE, *Chasseur*
Regiment
Voltigeur du 1. Bataillon Colonial.

Pl. 181

Troupes Françaises.

A Paris chez Martinet, Libraire, rue du Coq N.°15 et 15

Officier de Chasseurs à Cheval
Volontaire du 1.ᵉʳ Régiment du Dép.ᵗ de la Seine

150/181.1

Pl. 187

Troupes Françaises.

DOUANES IMPÉRIALES,
Brigade à Pied

A Paris chez Martinet, Libraire, rue du Coq N.º 13 et 15

Pl. 188.

Troupes Françaises

DOUANES IMPÉRIALES,
Brigade à Cheval

A Paris chez Martinet, Libraire, rue du Coq N.º 15 et 15

A.Paris chez Martinet, Libraire, rue du Coq N° 15.

Dep. à la Bib. Imp.

Gendarme

GENDARME À PIED.

en 1813

À Paris, chez Martinet, Libraire rue du Coq N.º 13 et 15.

A Paris chez Martinet, Libraire, rue du Coq N°. 13 et 15.

Lancier gendarme

A.Paris, chez Martinet, rue du Coq N.° 15.   Dép. à la Bib. Imp.

INFANTERIE LÉGERE. *Chasseur*
Régiment
d'Ysembourg.

Pl. 268 *Troupes Françaises*

A Paris, chez Martinet, rue du Coq N.º 15.

Dep. à la Bib. Imp.

INFANTERIE LÉGERE. *Chasseur*
Troisième Régiment étranger.

Pl. 243. bis

Troupes Françaises.

A Paris chez Martinet, Libraire, rue du Coq, N.º 13 et 15.

Officier des Lanciers 9.ᵉ Rég.ᵗ
Compagnie d'Elite.

158/243.1

Pl. 279 bis   Troupes Françaises

Lancier 7.ᵉ Rég.
Compagnie D'Elite

A Paris chez Martinet, Libraire, rue du Coq. N.º 13 et 15.

Pl. 227

Troupes Françaises.

A Paris chez Martinet, Libraire rue du Coq, N.º 13 et 15.

Légion Portugaise
Chasseur.

Pl. 229   Troupes Françaises.

A Paris chez Martinet, Libraire, rue du Coq, N°13 et 15.

LÉGION PORTUGAISE,
Cavalerie,

A Paris chez Martinet Libraire rue du Coq N.º 13 et 15.

SUISSE   3. —   Régiment

Grenadier.

162/258.1

CAPTIONS TO THE PLATES

The commentaries which follow attempt to point out some of the more interesting aspects of the prints reproduced. As discussed in Footnote 14, each reproduction has two identifying numbers, both of which are used in the heading to the relevant commentary. The first denotes the order of its appearance in this book, while the second is the number assigned to the print by Martinet, albeit with one embellishment. For the purposes of creating the inventory of known prints in the *Troupes Françaises* series which is contained in Appendix C, this author has had to deal with the problem of multiple prints which bear the same identifying number. In such cases, the print which, in the judgment of this author, is the one most commonly associated with a particular Martinet number has been assigned that integer for the purposes of this volume. The other prints (which in reality bear the same number) are identified in this work by the addition of a decimal to the whole number (e.g., 57.1, 57.2, etc.).

The text of the heading to each commentary is this author's English translation of the original French caption for the relevant print.

1/180.1 [Napoleon I, Emperor and King]
This print is one of the contemporary illustrations which helped to create the image of Napoleon in bicorne hat and grey overcoat, which is now so familiar as to be a cliché. The other figures are probably intended to represent French Marshals, but, if that is the case, the sash of the officer in the foreground should be white and gold. Most copies of this print bear the caption shown in square brackets above, but (for obvious political reasons) the plate for this print was modified after the Second Restoration and the caption was eliminated. This reproduction therefore shows the later state of the print.

2/248 Marshal of the Empire
This print depicts the modified full dress of a Marshal on campaign. The shoulder-cords were worn only by those Marshals, such as Davout, Soult and Mortier, who held senior ranks in the Imperial Guard. The green ornament on the breast of the jacket is probably an attempt to depict the decoration of the Order of the Iron Crown, which was worn suspended from a green-and-yellow ribbon. Note the reproduction of the artist's signature in the lower left-hand corner.

3/197 Brigade General
According to the Staff Dress Regulations, the tricolor ostrich feather *panache* of this figure should be entirely sky-blue and his plume should be half red. In addition, his sash suffers from a colourist's error, because the narrow stripes visible under the sky-blue colouring should be gold. The more interesting figure in this print is the orderly, who appears to be a Hussar of the 9th Regiment. The clear view of the back of a Napoleonic light cavalryman with

full equipment makes this print almost unique among primary iconographic sources.

4/272.1 Aide-de-Camp

The sky-blue plume and armband mark this figure as the aide to a Brigade General. The caption, however, uses the term '*Mestre de Camp*' (literally 'Camp Master'), a rank designation used under the Restoration, which indicates that this print was annotated post-1814. The composition of the single-unit print reminds the viewer of the mundane reality that even an elegant Napoleonic ADC had to worry about losing his hat at the full gallop.

5/234 Captain Attached to the General Staff

The undress uniform of a staff attaché was identical in style with that of an Adjutant-Commandant but the lace was limited to two pieces on each side of the collar and a Captain had a full epaulet on his left shoulder only. The Staff Dress Regulations specify blue breeches and a hat without plume, but both these points are obviously contradicted here.

6/192 War Commissary

The full dress uniform of this administrative officer of the *Grande Armée* conforms perfectly to the specifications set out in the Staff Dress Regulations, including the black goat's wool trim on the hat, the horizontal pockets and the heavy cavalry-style boots. The colour of the coat is presumably the sky-blue called for by the regulations, but it is obviously darker in shade than many modern versions of this colour.

7/210 Sub-Inspector of Reviews

The colourist has failed to paint the single row of silver lace that this figure should have on both his collar and cuffs, but otherwise this full dress uniform is accurately depicted. Its most unusual feature is the green sash with sil-ver fringe, which would have been sky-blue for a full Inspector and red for a Chief Inspector. The background of this print is full of detail, but the horse has the wrong horse furniture for this figure because it is red instead of sky-blue as required by Staff Dress Regulations.

8/250 Surgeon 1st Class

All medical officers of the French Army were supposed to wear the style of uniform with the gold lace across the chest shown in this print, but it looks distinctly unsuitable for combat wear. Distinctions among the various branches of the medical services were created by the facing colour displayed on the collar, cuffs and vest, which was red for surgeons, black for physicians and dark green for pharmacists. The uniform of this figure lacks the expected red vest, and its colour is darker and less green than the term *bleu barbeau* (light bluish-green) used in the regulations would suggest. The soldier on the right side of the print appears to be a Light Infantry Carabinier (post-1809).

9/58 Imperial Guard, Mounted Grenadier

Maleuvre, the artist whose name appears in the lower right-hand corner of this print, probably saw the Mounted Grenadiers on duty in Paris dozens of times, and was therefore able to capture even the smallest details of their full dress uniform, such as the red rosettes in the tail and mane of the horse and the brass grenade worked into the hilt of the sabre. The only odd touches are the lack of red trim to the saddlecloth and the fact that the width of the inner stripe of *aurore* lace on the saddlecloth and the holsters is not twice the width of the outer stripe. The artist has even gone so far as to depict the holes in the hooves caused by the horseshoe nails. The crown in the corner of the saddlecloth suggests a post-1807 date for this print.

10/184 Imperial Guard, Officer of Mounted Grenadiers

This officer has holsters with a three-piece cloth covering, thereby confirming that the officers and men of this regiment had different patterns of this piece of equipment. The horse furniture is also distinguished by a white instead of light brown leather saddle. The uniform is identical to that of the preceding trooper except for the colour gold replacing light orange for the trim, shoulder-cords and other ornaments. The belt plate is rather plain for an officer, being closer to the model used by the rank and file of the unit.

11/57 Imperial Guard, Dragoon

The similarities between the Guard Dragoon and Guard Mounted Grenadier uniforms are significant, the primary differences being those of jacket colour and head-dress. In addition, the holster cover of the Dragoon has three rather than two and the outer band of trim on the horse furnishings for the Dragoon is broader than the inner band, which is the reverse of the arrangement for the Mounted Grenadiers. Many sources show Guard Dragoons with red plumes, but this is certainly not the case here.

12/225 Dragoons of the Imperial Guard, Officer

The red plume indicates that this figure is a combat officer and not a member of the regimental staff, who would wear a white plume as a distinguishing mark. It is difficult to tell whether there are two or three rows of gold lace on the saddlecloth and holster covers, but Rousselot states in his Plate No. 13 that the latter number was correct for senior officers. Very few sources present a clear view of the underside of the horse furniture of a Napoleonic cavalryman, so this view of the white surcingle with coloured stripes is quite noteworthy.

13/230 Dragoons of the Imperial Guard, Trumpeters, Full and Ordinary Dress

The white uniform shown here was probably the second style of dress worn by the Trumpeters of the Guard Dragoons, the first (worn from 1807 to 1809) having included a sky-blue jacket. The horse hair 'tail' of the helmet worn with the first uniform was white, so the black tail shown here might represent either a change in that feature (necessitated by the lack of contrast between a white tail and the white cloth of the coat) and/or an error by the colourist. This print is the only primary iconographic source depicting the ordinary sky-blue uniform worn by the standing figure.

14/259.1 Dragoon of the Imperial Guard in Ordinary Dress

The substitution of hat for helmet and green trousers for white breeches gives this outfit a much different appearance from the full dress uniform of the Guard Dragoons. The differences are enhanced by the wearing of the standard waist belt over the shoulder. The colourist has apparently forgotten to include the cockade on the hat.

15/56 Imperial Guard, Elite Gendarme

Because there were only four companies of Elite Gendarmes attached to the Imperial Guard, and because they were primarily a security rather than a combat unit, there are few contemporary illustrations of their appearance. This is one of the best. Among the most distinctive features of the Gendarme uniform were the visor on the bearskin cap, the buff shoulder-belts trimmed with white and the buff vest and trousers. In contrast to the style of the Dragoons and the Mounted Grenadiers, the aiguilettes of the Elite Gendarmes were worn on the left shoulder.

16/291 Imperial Guard, Officer of Elite Gendarmes

The Elite Gendarmes were the only unit of Guard heavy cavalry whose officers were distinguished by silver lace and cords. This officer wears his aiguilette on the opposite shoulder from his troopers, thus allowing for the correct placement of his epaulette. The print correctly depicts him mounted on a black horse, but the absence of grenade ornaments in the turnbacks may be an oversight.

17/53 Imperial Guard, Mounted Chasseurs

Artistically, this appears to be one of the weaker prints in the Martinet series, because both the saddlecloth and the sword belt have been inaccurately depicted. (They are smaller than they should be.) But this work conveys a massive amount of accurate information about the full dress Guard Chasseur uniform. The print also presents three novel details. First, the green-and-red barrel sash one would expect to find around the Chasseur's waist is missing. Second, the doeskin breeches have been depicted with similarly coloured Hungarian knot decoration on the front of the thigh. Finally, the ornament on the breast strap of the saddle appears to be an eagle rather than a more standard brass heart or hunting-horn.

18/185 Imperial Guard, Mounted Chasseur in Ordinary Dress

The bicorne hat of this exquisitely drawn figure suggests that he has been depicted wearing town (or off-duty) dress (*tenue de ville*) rather than the so-called *petite* (literally 'little'), or ordinary dress, uniform. The colourist has omitted the red trim which should adorn the edge of the lapel next to the collar. The colour of the hat cords, aiguillette and Hungarian knot decorations on the breeches appear golden-yellow rather than light orange (or *aurore*), the colour called for by regulation.

The cuff has three buttons although most sources show only two. The background is fascinating, with the details of the street lamp being of particular interest.

19/231 Imperial Guard, Officer of Guides (Ordinary Dress)

The caption to this print is peculiar because it uses the archaic name for Napoleon's Guard Chasseurs. The picture has the feel of a portrait because of the arrogant bearing of the subject. The decorated blade of his sabre seems too curved to fit in the scabbard, but the scabbard itself is perfectly detailed down to the notch at its mouth. The light cavalry bridle and harness are also accurately depicted. Note the end of the holster sticking out from beneath the saddlecloth.

20/262 Officer of Mounted Chasseurs of the Guard

This print provides a remarkable comparison and contrast with the preceding picture, showing as it does the colourful hussar-style full dress uniform of the Chasseurs. It is well-established that many affluent officers did affect a leopard-skin saddlecloth, but the details of the lace and edging trim shown here are unique. The full dress bridle and harness, which sparkle with gilt ornaments, provide some measure of the accuracy of the Martinet prints because there is an almost identical Chasseur bridle in the French Army Museum.

21/290 Trumpeter of the Chasseurs of the Guard

This is one of only a very few contemporary depictions of a trumpeter of the Guard Chasseurs, so every bit of information it conveys is precious. Among the details of greatest significance are the dark fur trim on the pelisse (in contrast to the white fur of the bearskin cap), the dark red colour and embroidered decoration of the trumpet banner, the interlocking ring design for the edging to the saddlecloth and the red, blue and gold sabretache. Rousselot argues in his Plate No. 23 on Chasseur Trumpeters that lace of this figure should be mixed gold and crimson, but he cites no definitive authority for his conclusion. He also concludes that the valise should not have gold lace decorating its ends.

22/158 Imperial Guard, Mameluke

Much of what we know about the uniform of the Mamelukes after they had become somewhat westernised and standardised comes from the wealth of detail in this print. The artist has presented the horseman in the act of turning, so the trim on the front of the vest can be seen together with the arrangement of the dagger and the holster tucked into the blue waist sash. But he has not made a very skilful job of depicting the cords for the scabbard of the scimitar; they are very thick where they join the scabbard, but unnaturally thin where they run over the right shoulder and under the left arm of the figure. Variants: The Brown Collection alone has multiple versions of this print in which the long-sleeved shirt is, alternately, purple, blue and green.

23/100 Polish Light Horse of the Guard

There are many gaps in the existing information about the uniform worn by the Poles when they first joined the Imperial Guard, but it is possible that some of them are answered by this print. In the lower left-hand corner of the engraving, the date 1806 has been penned over the engraved signature 'Maleuvre', so this print may actually represent a member of the Polish Honour Guard which greeted Napoleon in Warsaw in December 1806. This would explain the novel features which appear in this print, but nowhere else in the iconogra-

phy of the unit: (1) lapels with laced buttonholes, but no exterior trim; (2) a full epaulette on the same shoulder as the aiguillette; (3) white trim to the saddlecloth. Note the handwritten title to this print, and the peculiar use of the spelling 'Polonois' instead of 'Polonais'.

24/205.1 Lancer of the Guard, 1st Regiment

This Original Version print was probably created in late 1809 or early 1810 following the Wagram campaign in which the Poles earned the right to use the lance as their weapon of choice. The uniform seen here is consistent with known regulations and other primary sources except for the absence of decoration on either the front flap or the trailing edge of the saddlecloth. The colour of the facings gives definitive proof that 'Polish' crimson was of a distinctly pink shade.

25/206 Imperial Guard, Kettle-Drummer of the Polish Lancers

There is no more fantastic figure in Napoleon's Grand Army than the single kettle-drummer of the Polish Lancers of the Guard. The uniform is oriental in cut – flowing white caftan, baggy trousers, red boots – but the profuse gold trim on the saddlecloth and drum banners is a distinctly baroque touch. The most exotic note of all, however, is struck by the unusual bridle and headstall. Lucien Rousselot's research has established that the Polish Lancers did not have a kettle-drummer until late 1810.

26/217 Officer of the Polish Lancers of the Guard in 1810

As might be expected, this officer wears essentially the same uniform as that worn by the rank-and-file lancers, although with silver trim and an impressive silver sash. (The sash, which was a parade dress item, and shown by only one other contemporary source, probably had some crimson stripes or checks.) The engraving includes the outline of the distinctive wave pattern of lace trim around the lapels and the collar, a feature unique to the 1st Guard Lancers, but the colourist has failed to make it silver as should have been the case. The full dress uniform is completed by crimson trousers in place of the blue ones used for ordinary wear.

27/251 Imperial Guard, Lancer, 2nd Regiment

The uniform of the so-called Dutch Lancers of the Guards was nearly identical in style with that of the 1st Regiment, but differed significantly in terms of colour. Some modern experts have argued that the arrangement of the colours of the lance pennon should be reversed and that the yellow epaulette on the right shoulder should have a blue crescent, but there is no reason to believe that this primary source is inaccurate on these points. Indeed, Rousselot's research has confirmed that another controversial point about this print is correct. Most modern sources state that the saddlecloth had a yellow 'N' decoration as well as the eagle shown here, but relevant procurement contracts mention only the latter item.

28/252 Officer of the Lancers of the Guard, 2nd Regiment

This print represents one case in which a multi-unit plate is not at all misleading because the only differences in dress between the two regiments of Guard Lancers were in fact ones which could be addressed by the print colourist. For instance, the lapel trim for the Polish Lancer officer has simply been obliterated here by the dark blue of the lapel. Note that Guard Lancer officers wore the aiguilette on the opposite shoulder from their troops.

29/292.2 Honour Guard, 3rd Regiment

The only feature distinguishing this unit from the other three regiments of Honour Guards is the yellow plume tip. (The colour of the pompon is also yellow, but that is coincidental since it represents a squadron, as opposed to regimental, distinction.) The colour of the dolman, pelisse and plume seems more black than green, but the latter colour is undoubtedly the one intended. The colourist has failed to paint in the crimson barrels of the hussar-style sash worn around the waist. One unique, debatable detail is that the sleeves of the pelisse have distinct red cuffs.

30/52 Imperial Guard, Foot Grenadier

This is the classic Napoleonic infantryman in summer full dress (the season being indicated by his white gaiters). This print captures fine details such as the line of stitching along each edge of the shoulder-belts and the intricacies of the butt of the musket facing the viewer, but it inexplicably omits the lowest cuff flap button on each sleeve.

31/117 Imperial Guard Grenadier and Cantinière

This print is precious for two reasons: it shows the back of a Guard Grenadier's uniform, and the costume worn by a camp-follower of the period (described literally in this case as a 'Female Seller of Brandy following the Army'). The woman's dress is exceedingly sensible and modest, with a hint of colour suggesting both a scarf at her throat and a kerchief around her head. The dog presumably belongs to her. The rear view of the Grenadier reveals such details as the two buttons at the small of the back and the outward-facing flames of the grenades on the cartridge box. Note that this figure does not have his hair arranged in a queue.

32/266 Imperial Guard, Foot Grenadier Officer

The confident bearing of this figure once again suggests that element of portraiture (or, indeed, caricature) is occasionally found in Martinet prints. The uniform is perfectly accurate except for the lack of a blue centre for the cockade (which is present in other versions of this print). The sabre is definitely not a regulation pattern item, but there is no reason to believe that it has been inaccurately depicted.

33/120 Imperial Guard, Grenadier Sapper

This Sapper's uniform and equipment include many traditional features such as the crossed-axe badge on his arm, the short musket slung over his shoulder and the sabre with hilt shaped like the head of a rooster. He also has a particularly bushy beard, which was another distinguishing mark of his office. There is some paint on the upper surface of the figure's left epaulet which suggests that the colourist was trying to indicate some special feature (brass metal trim?), but the result is enigmatic.

34/214.1 Imperial Guard, Grenadier, 3rd Regiment

At the dissolution of his brother's Kingdom of Holland, Napoleon imported the 3rd, or Dutch, Grenadiers into the Imperial Guard, but they retained their exotic Dutch uniforms. An earlier state of this print shows the same figure with the yellow/orange buttonhole lace worn by the unit before its incorporation into the French Army. In this print state, that earlier detail has been eliminated, but the task was botched because the engraver also removed all the lapel buttons at the same time. Note that this figure, unlike other Guard infantrymen depicted in the series, is wearing a queue.

35/269 Imperial Guard, Grenadier Officer, 3rd Regiment

At first glance this figure appears to be a multi-subject print based on the same plate as Print No. 32/266 because the images seem identical down to the shadows on the ground. Close examination of details such as the gaiters and the way the gloves are held reveals, however, that this print is actually based on distinct, if similar, artwork. The shading on the leg, the shape of the cross of the *Légion d'honneur* and, most of all, the reconfiguration of the bearskin and its cording to reflect the fact that the Dutch Grenadiers did not wear a cap plate all give a telling indication of the amount of artistic effort that went into each Martinet offering.

36/54 Imperial Guard, Foot Chasseurs

The classic elegance of the summer full dress uniform of the Guard Foot Chasseurs is faithfully captured in this print with the exception of the lack of white trim around the edges of the cuffs. A detail of Chasseur dress that is found only in this print is the existence of the three large buttons below the right lapel. Such buttons were a routine feature of line infantry uniforms, but no other source documents their use on a light infantry-style jacket with pointed lapels.

37/107 Officer of Chasseurs of the Imperial Guard

This figure appears to be wearing a service, rather than a full dress, uniform because he is wearing black riding-boots with a brown 'cuff'. Once again, there is no white trim on the jacket cuff, although this detail is found in almost all other sources. The wearing of a gorget by this figure raises an interesting speculative point as to why this object does not appear in other prints of officers.

38/62 Imperial Guard, Fusilier

It is impossible to identify with certainty which of the several units of Guard Fusiliers is depicted in this print, but circumstantial evidence such as the pointed lapels and the recurring use of a green and red colour combination suggests that the intention was to represent a member of the Fusilier–Chasseur regiment formed in 1806. There are other states of this print in which the figure has a longer plume, pointed cuffs with white trim (and no cuff flaps) and red epaulettes with a green shoulder-piece.

39/172 Imperial Guard, Fusilier-Grenadier
There is a another state of this print in the Brunon Collection which displays some material differences from this figure: white cuff flaps, a red tassel on the sword strap and no buttons at all below the left lapel. The absence of white stripes on the shoulder-piece of the epaulet may be an error of the colourist because this feature is widely noted in other sources. A last interesting point about this print is the single button of unknown purpose on the trousers just below the vest.

40/118 Imperial Guard, Tirailleur
There seem to be more versions of this multi-subject print (and its companion, Print No. 121) than of any other infantry prints in the series, a fact which is a tribute to the variety and number of units created by Napoleon for his so-called Young Guard. Moreover, a great many of these versions depict uniforms which flatly contradict the information provided by other contemporary sources. For instance, the uniform in this print is generally consistent with that described in the Tirailleur's organisational decree of 10 March 1809, but that document specifies a red collar, blue ornaments for the turnbacks and blue shoulder-straps.

41/118.1 Imperial Guard, Tirailleur Voltigeur
The Voltigeurs of the Guard were not formed until 1810, when the Tirailleur–Chasseurs were given a new unit title. These units had

the same basic uniforms as the Tirailleurs (but did not have that name in their official title), except that the collar was yellow, the shoulder-straps were green (trimmed white, according to many sources) and the turnback ornaments were green hunting-horns instead of blue eagles. The cuffs should have white trim.

42/121.1 Imperial Guard, Tirailleur, Conscript Grenadiers
The name of the Conscript Grenadiers suggests a contradiction in terms, but it demonstrates the lengths to which Napoleon was prepared to go to entice more enthusiasm from his soldiers by giving them special status. This depiction includes a number of features (the pointed lapels, the lack of red trim around the lapels, the pointed cuffs and the white trim for the pockets) for the uniform of this unit that are not found in other sources.

43/176 Imperial Guard, Drum Major
This print is one of the two contemporary sources that depict the Drum Major of the Imperial Guard Grenadiers (the other being another, less artistic, commercial print published in Paris). The lavish use of gold lace was a traditional feature of all Drum Major uniforms, but the embroidery shown here is particularly elaborate, as would be fitting for the leading figure in all Guard parades. The use of heron feathers accounts for the distinctive shape of the plume. The tentative red colouring of the collar may be a mistake on the part of the colourist because French Grenadier units of the Guard all had blue collars. The elaborate baldric is shown worn over the right shoulder, but this arrangement is reversed in most modern sources.

44/244 Imperial Guard, Musician of the Foot Grenadiers
This print is the foremost primary source for information about the uniforms of the magnif-

icent band of the Imperial Guard Grenadiers. This is surprising because the band of some 45 professional musicians (as opposed to soldiers) was, to the populace of Napoleon's capital city, one of the most visible and impressive symbols of his regime.

45/289 Imperial Guard, Flanker

The Regiment of Flankers, which was created by a decree dated 4 September 1811, was a specialist unit recruited from the sons and nephews of employees of Napoleon's forestry guards. The only other contemporary illustration of this unit is a print by Weiland which depicts a uniform with a green collar and green cuffs, all piped yellow, and without the red transverse strip across the shoulder-strap. The bottom of the jacket is drawn in an odd manner so that the red line looks more like a part of the lining than the turnback it should represent.

46/213 Foot Artilleryman of the Guard

It is possible to date this print with some accuracy because, prior to May 1810, the head-dress of the Guard artillery was the shako rather than the bearskin with visor shown in this picture. The rear view of the second figure gives unique information about the patch on the crown of the bearskin, and also reveals that the red cords were only worn across the front. The rest of the uniform had nothing to distinguish it from that of the line artillery except for the red epaulettes.

47/198 Horse Artilleryman of the Guard

The wide-eyed figure staring down at the shell about to explode at his feet gives a manic touch to this print. There are no details other than the blue saddle cloth to confirm that this figure is a member of the Imperial Guard, because the dress uniforms of both Line and Guard horse artillery were almost identical.

The colourist has certainly made two mistakes: the yellow 'barrels' of the barrel sash have not been coloured in, and the face of the sabretache has been left blank. It is less clear whether the blue patch where the shoulder-belt crosses the shoulder is a mistake or is intended to be a shoulder-strap.

48/36.1 Horse Artilleryman in ordinary dress

Although the caption is silent on this point, the Guard status of this figure is confirmed by the aiguilette on his left shoulder. The only detail that seems questionable is the fact that the sword knot is all white instead of white with a red tassel, as for the Grenadiers of the Guard. This is a multi-subject print which is linked to Print No. 18/185, but the colouring in this case is appropriate for the artillery arm.

49/270 Imperial Guard, Horse Artillery Officer

This is one of the more artistically adept prints in the series. The white fur trim on the pelisse, the design of the sabretache (which lacks the laurel branch decoration found on each side of the eagle in many surviving examples of this item) and the leopard-skin saddle cloth are the most impressive details of this uniform, but the most interesting may be the way in which the two cap cord raquettes are suspended from a gold wire (?) loop instead of from the cap cords themselves.

50/238.1 Ex-Guard Train in 1813

Despite the date in the caption to this print, the uniform it depicts corresponds most closely to the description of the uniform which came into use for the Guard Artillery Train in late 1809–10. This possibility is reinforced by the fact that the scarlet lace on the shako, the braided waistcoat and hussar-style trousers and boots are more typical of the earlier period. The shoulder-strap appears to have a trefoil ending and a blue trimmed red shoulder-piece. Prints such as these and the one following provide important information about the colour 'iron-grey' in Napoleonic uniforms.

51/101 Imperial Guard, Train

This print depicts another type of uniform of the Guard Artillery Train. The shape of the shako plate and the lack of adornment for the shako itself suggest that this uniform can be dated to 1812–13. The colour of the shako plate and the visor trim is consistent with the colour of the uniform buttons, but these details are contrary to all other information we have about the dress of that unit. One expert has tried to explain the white vest and trousers, and the heavy cavalry-style boots, by saying that they are part of the campaign uniform for this unit, while another has argued that the figure is actually a member of the Guard Equipment Train.

52/253 Imperial Guard, Engineer Sapper

A company of Sappers was added to the Guard by a decree dated 10 July 1810. Their purpose was to provide fire-fighting protection to imperial palaces and residences by manning mobile water pumps. The exotic aspect of their uniform was provided by a massive steel helmet similar to that worn by the Carabiniers.

53/267 Imperial Guard, Officer of Engineer Sappers.

It is easier to see the details of the eagle plate of the Sapper helmet in this print than in the preceding illustration. Although there is one, often-reproduced drawing of the decorative helmet plate which includes a profusion of thunderbolts gripped in the talons of the eagle, this is not the case here nor on the example of the Sapper helmet owned by the Museum of the Army in Paris. In the background can be seen the rear view of the uniform of a rank-and-file Sapper.

54/61 Imperial Guard, Sailor

The figure in this print is dressed in an early version of the full dress uniform of the Guard Sailors because, some time after 1805, all models of Dolman had five rows of buttons instead of the three shown here. In fact, Rousselot reports having seen later states of this print to which two extra rows of buttons have been added. The special models of the sabre and the brass epaulettes of the Sailors are accurately rendered, but the Eagle plate for the shako seems undersized and the base of the plume seems unduly thick.

55/104.1 Mounted Carabinier, 2nd Regiment in 1807

Since the only difference between the 1st and 2nd Carabinier Regiments was in the colour of their cuff flaps, the gloves on this figure prevent a verification of the unit designation in the print caption. The cylindrical shape of the saddle-pack dates the print to 1808 or later even though the saddlecloth lacks the second, narrow interior line of white lace which also came into to use in 1808. Other noteworthy points are the length of the musket, the absence of a sheepskin cover for the saddle and the way in which the cartridge box hangs loose over the folded cloak.

56/294 Mounted Carabinier, — Regiment

This print presents a remarkably accurate picture of the post-1810 Carabinier uniform. The only problem is that the white metal border of the cuirass is not correctly depicted, and one might quibble as well about the inappropriately exaggerated red lining for the chin scales and for the shoulder-pieces of the breast plate. The dark shade of sky-blue used for the facings is consistent with the colour that appears in many other contemporary paintings of this uniform.

57/295 Mounted Carabinier Officer

Since there is no doubt that the body armour for Carabinier officers was copper plated, the breast plate and helmet of this figure should be less yellow than they have been coloured in this instance. In addition, the depiction of the cuirass is inaccurate in three ways: there is no wide band of silver metal around the edge, the shoulder-straps are too thin and have too wide a lining, and the silver plate on the breast of the plate should be decorated with a copper star, and not a face. The model of sabre is highly unusual.

58/216 Cuirassier Trumpeter, 1st Regiment

The colour of this trumpeter's jacket is, by comparison with the dark blue saddle cloth, definitely a shade of dark sky-blue. Commandant Bucquoy theorised that an association between this colour and the 1st Cuirassiers could be inferred from the fact that Colonel Clerc, the unit's commander in 1809, came from the Guard Chasseurs, whose trumpeters did wear sky-blue. Bucquoy also provides the startling information that he was aware of a total of five different coloured states for this print (one with a dark blue jacket, one with a red jacket, and three with the sky-blue jacket, including one with yellow lace). Such diversity makes it difficult to rely on any one version.

59/113 Cuirassiers, 4th Regiment

The 4th Regiment of Cavalry was not transformed into Cuirassiers until 1804. As with all the Type I Cuirassier multi-subject prints, it is impossible to confirm the regimental designation specified for this figure in the caption because the cuffs of the jacket are not visible.

60/204 Cuirassier Trumpeter, 4th Regiment

Because this is the first print numerically in the Martinet series to depict a Cuirassier trumpeter, it is possible that it is the Original Version for all the Type IV Cuirassier Trumpeter prints and therefore was actually based on direct observation of a trumpeter of the 4th Regiment. If that were the case, this multi-subject print could be considered more accurate for this unit than for any other. In any event, the solid red uniform with white lace is striking. Note the red strap trimmed with white which is used to keep the waist belt in place.

61/86.2 Cuirassiers, 5th Regiment

This Type II Cuirassier Print is one of the very few primary illustrations of Napoleonic uniforms that confirm that some Cuirassier regiments actually did wear uniforms faced with the new facing colours such as the *aurore* (light orange) described by the 1812 Regulations.

62/45 Cuirassiers, 7th Regiment

There is a bit of scallop-shaped trim at the bottom of the breast plate of this figure which seems to suggest that the lining of his cuirass was yellow, but that detail is extremely questionable.

63/209 Cuirassiers, Superior Officer, 7th Regiment

The amount and shape of silver trim on the saddle cloth of this Type III Cuirassier print looks very similar to that depicted by Nicolas Hoffman in his print of the Colonel (*Chef de Brigade*) of the 10th Cuirassiers *circa* 1804. The narrow width of the coat tails is also unusual, but such exaggerated features were sometimes considered a very fashionable touch.

64/240 Cuirassier Trumpeter, 7th Regiment

The startling novelty of the sky-blue lace on the uniform of this trumpeter is perhaps the best indicator that this feature may be accurate. Given the generally high reliability of the prints in the *Troupes Françaises* series, it is difficult to imagine such a depiction being tolerated if it was, in fact, incorrect. Accentuating the novelty of this Type IV Cuirassier print are the white sheepskin saddle cover with yellow edging and the sky-blue saddle cloth. Another unusual feature is the red (instead of yellow) lining to the trumpeter's white cloak folded on top of his saddle cloth.

65/153 Cuirassiers, 13th Regiment

The facing colour of the 13th Regiment was the unique, and evocatively named, shade known as '*lie de vin*' (wine dregs). The sombre aspect of that colour perhaps accounts for the fact that the grenade ornament in the turnbacks is white trimmed blue rather than solid blue.

66/89.1 Dragoon Corporal, 4th Regiment, Departure from Cantonment

This print presents the second state of the Type VII Dragoon Print. The figure is wearing the precise uniform colours prescribed for his unit in the 1812 Regulations down to the vertical pockets in the short jacket tails. There are, however, a few unusual omissions – there are no grenade ornaments in the turnbacks and no regimental numbers on either the saddle cloth or the portmanteau. (Coincidentally, Carle Vernet's 1812 painting of a trooper of the 4th for the Bardin Regulations confirms both these points.) The grenade ornament on the cartridge box is a detail unique to this print Type.

67/163 Dragoon Officer, 6th Regiment

Martinet's colourists generally had a great deal of difficulty representing the colour silver, which is why it often ends up as the indistinct grey shade used for the grenade ornaments of this figure's turnbacks. According to the 1801 Equipment Specifications, the holster covers of Dragoon officers had only two, rather than three, parts.

68/36.2 Light Cavalry, Dragoon, Elite Company, 7th Regiment

This Type V Dragoon print demonstrates that the colours crimson and scarlet are odd bedfellows in the same uniform colour scheme. The brass chin-strap for the bearskin is noteworthy, as is the use of white cords with the red plume. However, in his Plate No. 86: *Dragons, Complément 1804–1815*, Rousselot states that this colour combination was also used by the elite companies of the 1st, 8th and 19th Dragoons.

69/178 Dragoon Officer, 14th Regiment, Colonel

The Colonel of the 14th Dragoons from 1806 to 1810 was Joseph Bouvier des Eclaz (1757–1830), a veteran of more than 30 years service, so it would seem that this Type VI Dragoon print is not an exact portrait of that officer. The rich uniform of this figure features gilding of the helmet, sabre hilt and belt buckle as well as a second row of silver lace on the saddle cloth and the holster cover.

70/85 Light Cavalry, Dragoon, 17th Regiment

There is no record of any Dragoon of the 17th Regiment actually participating in the capture of an English standard although the regiment was present at the Battle of Albuera (16 May 1811) when that feat was performed four times. Although white plumes were typically reserved for staff personnel in other branches of the military, they were apparently quite common for all members of Dragoon regiments. Green is an unusual colour for Dragoon turnback ornaments.

71/166.1 Dragoon Officer, 19th Regiment

The depiction of the horizontal pocket in the tail of the uniform jacket of this figure demonstrates once again the high level of accuracy to be found even in multi-subject prints of the Martinet series such as this Type IV origination. The knob protruding from the top of the holster cover is, presumably, the butt of a pistol, but it was certainly not recognised and painted as such by the colourist.

72/97 Light Cavalry, Dragoon, 22nd Regiment

The 22nd Regiment had vertical pockets which seem to be missing from the coat tails of this figure. The regimental number, which appears on both the saddlecloth and the end of the portmanteau, should be white instead of silver. The red plume is probably a regimental distinction. As in all the other prints of Dragoon troopers in the *Troupes Françaises* series, the shoulder-strap button is positioned in the centre of the end of the strap farthest from the collar.

73/79 Light Cavalry, Dragoon, 25th Regiment

The most significant point of interest in this Type I Dragoon print is the red-over-black plume. As with the preceding print, the regimental numbers (and the grenade ornaments in the turnbacks) should be white instead of silver/grey. The jacket is missing its prescribed horizontal pocket. This print and the next two provide fresh and important visual information about the appearance of the colour *aurore* (light orange).

74/183 Light Cavalry, Dragoon, Elite Company, 28th Regiment in 1810

The figure here differs from some other versions of the Type V Dragoon print in the use of white epaulets to complete the distinctions for the elite company of the unit. His dress is unremarkable except that according to the 1812 Regulations the collar should have been *aurore* instead of green. This figure is missing the pocket which should be standard for a Dragoon of this type.

75/37 Light Cavalry, Dragoon, 29th Regiment

The exposed cuff of this figure allows for the one definitive regimental identification in the sequence of Dragoon prints, since such identification is impossible unless the collar, cuffs and pockets of the relevant uniform are visible. The colourist has confused the cartridge box with the saddle behind it and thus outlined the box in brown in a way which highlights its design. The star-shaped boss connecting the chin-strap to the helmet can be seen more clearly here than in other prints.

76/257 Dragoon, Stable Dress, Morning Grooming

This image beautifully illustrates the mundane side of Napoleonic military life which is overlooked by many sources. The stable jacket, loose-fitting trousers and wooden shoes are all eminently practical articles. The most unusual feature is the stable cap. It is certainly closer in design to the 1812/1813 'pokalem' cap than to the earlier forage cap with its long stocking top, but the concentric circles ornamenting the top of the cap are unique. The details of the stable itself are also uniquely interesting.

77/189.1 Mounted Chasseur Officer, 2nd Regiment

The dress of the Chasseur branch of Napoleon's light cavalry was certainly less flamboyant than that of the Hussars, but it was equally elegant in a more subdued way. This elite company officer wears the characteristic fur *colback*, or busby, with a red plume. Martinet's Type II Chasseur prints are the only source that indicate a double (as opposed to single) stripe of lace along the side seam of the breeches.

78/73.1 Mounted Chasseurs, 3rd Regiment

This Type III Chasseur print has been customised in the colouring process to represent an elite company trooper dressed in an 1812-style jacket with full lapels. To achieve this result the colourist has painted a busby over the engraved shako and added a line of silver buttons to indicate the edge of the lapel. He has not, however, added the line of coloured piping called for by the 1812 Regulations. The wholly green plume is unusual.

79/65 Mounted Chasseurs, 5th Regiment

The 5th Chasseurs were easy to identify in the field because they wore yellow leather belts and gloves. They wore dolmans almost until the end of the First Empire, and retained longer than all other regiments the 'wing' style of shako (i.e., a shako wrapped with a strip of cloth that was black on one side and coloured on the other; either side could be displayed depending on the state of dress to be worn). The line across the front of the head-dress in this print seems to have been an attempt to depict the existence of a wing in this case. The orange colour of the barrels in the barrel sash and the trim to the sheepskin saddle cloth is clearly not an error (because the colourist certainly had yellow paint), but it does defy easy explanation.

80/181 Mounted Chasseur Officer, 6th Regiment

The bright yellow facings and the scarlet belts of this figure contrast vividly with the predominantly green background of his uniform. In fact, the scarlet colour is probably too bright to represent accurately the shade of red leather belting worn by fashionable First Empire officers. The white plume suggests that this print depicts a member of the regimental staff rather than an officer attached to a line squadron.

81/43.1 Mounted Chasseurs, 7th Regiment

This print seems to be a later state of the Type III Chasseur print which is distinguished by

the fact that the back visor of the shako has been eliminated, and some additional shadow and detail has been added to the background (including a second window for the house on the horizon). The shako still has a simple cockade rather than a plate, but this is consistent with detail in other contemporary sources relating to several Chasseur regiments, including the 7th. The yellow metal chin-strap and visor trim are unique touches.

82/95 Mounted Chasseurs, 11th Regiment

Since the figure in this print is wearing gauntlets, the prescribed crimson facing colour of his uniform can only be seen at the base of the plume, in the barrels of his barrel sash and in the triangular trim to the saddle cloth. The shako plate is the standard diamond-shaped decoration first put into use in 1805–6. The hilt guard of the sabre is similar to that for the so-called 'Montmorency' sabre particular to the 2nd Chasseurs, but is of yellow rather than white metal.

83/51 Mounted Chasseurs, 16th Regiment

The shade of sky-blue used in this print is closer than any other used in the Martinet series to the light shade used in most modern works on Napoleonic military uniforms. This version differs from most other Type III Chasseur prints in that the portion of the scabbard hanging below the belly of the horse has been clearly coloured black with a brass tip. The 16th received new uniforms in mid-1809 to replace their old dolmans.

84/90 Mounted Chasseurs, 23rd Regiment

The uniform and equipment of this figure present a number of anomalous features. First, the piping on the collar and cuffs is white instead of green. Secondly, both the button on the shoulder-strap and that which should appear on the stomach just under his left arm have been omitted. Thirdly, the chin-strap of the shako is depicted as having been made of white metal, while the trim on both visors is yellow. Finally, the sword hilt is the correct shape, but the wrong colour, for the Year XI light cavalry sabre.

85/102 Mounted Chasseurs, 27th Regiment

The Belgian Light Horse commanded by the Duke of Aremburg was a short-lived unit which was transformed into the 27th Regiment of French Chasseurs in May 1808. Although one squadron wore a special hussar-style uniform, most of the regiment wore the more conventional dress shown in this print. The unit did, however, have the distinction of being the sole Chasseur unit to use yellow instead of white for trim and shako cords. The use of yellow leather belts and gloves is an additional plausible detail which is unique to this print. Other unusual features are the yellow trim on the figure's cuff and the *amaranthe* (dark crimson) trim on the end of the portmanteau.

86/6 Hussar, 1st Regiment

The sky-blue uniform of the Bercheny Hussars of the *ancien régime* bore red facings only on its cuffs, but by 1808 the successor 1st Hussars of Napoleon's *Grande Armée* had switched to red breeches as well. This innovation was never recorded in contemporary regulations, but several primary sources in addition to this Martinet print demonstrate its existence. The design of the sabretache matches perfectly with the design of some surviving examples of that piece of equipment. No colour has been applied to the portmanteau, which makes for an interesting view of the underlying engraving work. The dolmans of this Regiment typically had five rows of buttons.

87/128 Hussar Officer, 1st Regiment

The most striking contrast between this print and the preceding one of a trooper of the same regiment is to be found in the different shade of blue used to depict the sky-blue pelisse and dolman. The visual impact of the red breeches is diminished by the use of red leather for his boots and belts.

88/7 Hussar, 2nd Regiment

There are several unique points to the uniform depicted in this print. The first is the fact that the upper two-thirds of the plume are sky-blue. The second is that the background of the sabretache is red and the trim is yellow instead of white. The third is that the edging of the sheepskin saddle cloth is red instead of sky-blue.

89/8.2 Hussar, 3rd Regiment

This Type III Hussar print nicely illustrates the unique black belts and crimson braid of the 3rd Hussar Regiment. The basic colour of the uniform of this regiment bears the official name of *gris argentin* (silver-grey), but it has definite blue overtones in this print. The grey portmanteau with a crimson end is a noteworthy feature, as is the use of yellow rather than white metal numbers on the sabretache and portmanteau. The 3rd is another regiment which should have five rows of buttons on the dolman, not three.

90/150 Hussar Officer, 3rd Regiment

As with most Type IV Hussar Prints, there are no uniform features in this picture that can be said to be unique to the 3rd Hussars. The uniform colour is more grey and less blue than that of the figure in the preceding print.

91/10 Hussar, 4th Regiment

The uniform colours of the 4th Hussars are accurately captured in this print. This is an altered state of the Type I Hussar print because both the plate and the cords of the shako have been removed. There are several other primary sources which depict a sabre-tache with a single brass number on its face as the standard for this unit which also had five ranks of buttons on the dolman and pelisse.

92/11.1 Hussar, 5th Regiment

The sky-blue shako in this print is an oddity which is associated with 5th Hussar trumpeters by several sources. This print, however, is the only first-hand source that depicts use of this head-dress by a trooper of the regiment. The colour has been applied in a sufficiently light wash that one can make out the shako plate which has been coloured over. The colours of the sabretache are correct, but surviving examples of the model worn by the rank and file of this unit have a wreath around the centre number. White plumes, which were otherwise used primarily by staff personnel, were standard for this Regiment.

93/134 Hussar Officer, 5th Regiment

A private collection portrait of Colonel Meuziau of the 5th Hussars in 1810 was used by Rigo as the source for his *Le Plumet* Plate No. 245. A comparison of this print of a Hussar captain and that portrait (as reproduced by Rigo) reveals significant similarities between the uniforms and saddle furniture depicted. The portrait, however, depicts the colonel wearing an elaborately decorated shako instead of a busby, plain baggy trousers in lieu of hussar breeches, with elaborate braid and black (instead of red) belts. The sabretache colour and design are exactly the same in both sources, while the leopard-skins differ only in the colour of the outer trim (which is sky-blue in the portrait).

94/12 Hussar, 6th Regiment

The shape of this shako plate is accurate, but its colour is unexpected, since all other sources state that this item was made of the same yellow metal as the buttons of the uniform. A surviving brass example bears an embossed eagle resting on the numeral '6' cut into the plate as for a stencil. On the same theory, the shako cords should also be yellow. The design of the sabretache agrees generally with that depicted in other sources, but there should be a large yellow '6' in its centre. The red base to the black plume is noteworthy.

95/30 Hussar, 7th Regiment

The white plume with red tip on this trooper of the 7th is unique in primary source Hussar iconography, but otherwise his uniform depicts the expected array of colours, braid and equipment. The model of sabretache is correct, but the colours are not, it being reasonably well established that this Regiment carried a green sabretache with yellow trim and embroidery throughout the Napoleonic era.

96/31 Hussar, 8th Regiment

This Type II Hussar print is one of the few in the Martinet series to have a manuscript date in its caption. The 8th Hussars did have a red head-dress in the year noted, but it was most likely a tall cylindrical shako *rouleau*, and not the model depicted here. This combination illustrates how a Martinet colourist would deal with practical issues by using the image he had to hand (in this case, one showing a trooper with an early model of shako even if it was theoretically out of date). The 8th is thought to have switched from white to mixed red and green cords *circa* 1808, but the braid in this print seems to include an element of white. This might be a transitional style. The sabretache with shield and number fits perfectly the description of campaign model used by this unit, but other sources indicate that the metal decorations were silver like the uniform buttons.

97/32 Hussar, 9th Regiment

This print presents a very accurate depiction (up to and including the yellow tip of the black plume) of the uniform worn by this unit *circa* 1810. It also provides further evidence that the colour known as sky-blue during the Napoleonic Wars was darker than has been presumed by many modern authorities. Note that the colourist has added another row of buttons to the dolman in order to conform to the five button style worn by the unit.

98/33 Hussar, 10th Regiment

This print presents a second state of the Type II Hussar print in that the shako plate and bands have been removed from the basic engraving. The details of the plume and the sabretache have been customised in such a way as to suggest that the colourist was provided with accurate information about the dress of this unit. In particular, it is very interesting to note that Weiland's print of a trooper of the 10th has the same yellow metal shield on the sabretache, even though white metal would make more sense given the colour of the unit's buttons.

99/122 Hussar Officer, 10th Regiment

Moyle Scherer, a British officer serving with the 34th Foot in the Peninsula in 1811, was impressed by the uniform of the 10th Hussars: 'This corps wore a jacket and pelisse of light blue, or French grey, neatly ornamented with white lace and black fur; their caps, boots, and accoutrements, excellent; their hair clubbed in a manner not unbecoming; and their whole appearance soldier-like.' One wonders what Scherer might have had to say about the lavish uniform of this officer.

100/255 Hussar, 11th Regiment

The unit depicted in this print originated as the 2nd Hussars of the Dutch Army and were taken into French service when the Kingdom of Holland was dissolved. The distinguishing feature of its uniforms was the white fur trim on the pelisses. Several other primary sources note that the plain black sabretache with brass numerals was a regimental pattern.

101/296 Hussar, 12th Regiment

The 12th Hussar Regiment was created in 1813 by assigning a new number to the 9th *bis* (or Alternate 9th) Regiment, which had itself been created in 1812 by splitting the 9th Hussars into two separate units. This split was made in recognition of the fact that half the regiment was serving in Spain while half was about to participate in the Russian Campaign. The uniform of the 9th *bis* was distinguished from that of its parent by changing the colour of the dolman collar and cuffs to red and the colour of the lace to white. When the unit became the 12th, the collar and cuffs again became sky-blue. The green plume of this figure is unusual, as is the pattern of lace on the end of the portmanteau.

102/208.1 French Light Horse [Lancer], 1st Regiment

The 1st Regiment of French Light Horse Lancers was created in the summer of 1811 by means of a transformation of the 1st Dragoons. The unit number appearing on the end of the portmanteau would more likely have been of yellow wool braid rather than the yellow metal suggested here.

103/228.1 — Officer of French Light Horse [Lancers], 1st Regiment

This print may date from after the first Bourbon restoration because the 'N' which can be seen on the belt plate in other versions of this same print has been deliberately painted over. A comparison of this print with the preceding one highlights the greater elegance of the officer's helmet.

104/221.1 French Light Horse [Lancer], 2nd Regiment

The most significant feature of this print, which cannot be verified through any other source, is the use of the *aurore* facing colour in place of the more traditional yellow for the trim on the breeches and boots. The facing colour has also been used for the trim of the sheepskin saddle cloth. Note that the colourist forgot to colour the portion of the uniform jacket below the lance shaft.

105/260.1 Officer of French Light Horse [Lancers], 4th Regiment

This unit had the same crimson facing colour as the 9th Dragoons from which it was created. The star on the boss which attaches the chin-scales to the helmet has been carefully coloured crimson with a blue centre, but it is impossible to determine whether this represents a regimental distinction or is merely a flight of fancy on the part of the colourist.

106/264.1 Officer of French Light Horse [Lancers], 5th Regiment

The colour combination of sky-blue facings on a green uniform was worn by only one other Napoleonic regiment (the 16th Chasseurs). The facing colour used here appears to be more vivid than that used in the Martinet print for that other unit. This officer's sabre is shown as being made entirely of yellow metal, but this differs from the mixed gold and silver model shown in the preceding Type II Lancer Officer prints.

107/34 Line Infantry, 15th Regiment

Despite the manuscript notation under the caption to this print, the figure depicted is undoubtedly a Fusilier, and not a Voltigeur, because the uniform has shoulder-straps instead of epaulets and because the figure is wearing only a single equipment belt. The use of the black facing colour on this uniform follows exactly the White Uniform Regulations covering the white uniform experiment in 1806–7. Although the uniform has white metal buttons, the shako plate is brass. The circular yellow shako pompom and the yellow shako cords are both noteworthy.

108/34.1 Line Infantry, Chasseur, 15th Regiment in 1807

The caption on this print is also wrong, because the term 'Voltigeur' was used instead of 'Chasseur' to designate the light company of a line infantry regiment. The yellow collar and the green shako cords and epaulettes (with yellow crescent) are typical Voltigeur distinctions. Unlike the prior figure from the same regiment, this figure has white cuff flaps. His white gaiters were standard summer wear.

109/36 Line Infantry, Grenadier, 15th Regiment

The trio of prints illustrating the white uniforms worn by the 15th Line conclude with this classic Grenadier. The Hamburg Manuscript also has a print depicting a Grenadier from this unit in the white uniform, but that figure wears a shako with red cords. The White Uniform Regulations do not actually specify cuff flap colours for the relevant regiments, so variety in this item may have been the rule.

110/133.1 Line Infantry, 19th Regiment

The uniform of this Fusilier represents the typical dress of the majority of infantrymen in the French Army. The most noteworthy points are the 1810-model shako plate, the button securing the end of the shoulder-strap away from the shoulder and the closure of the cuff with two buttons (and no cuff flap).

111/5 Line Infantry, Grenadier, 32nd Regiment

The arrangement of the *capucine* facing colour on this depiction of the white uniform worn by the 32nd Line in 1807 corresponds exactly to that specified in the White Uniform Regulations. Those also provided, however, that the buttons of the 32nd should be silver rather than brass, which is probably the reason why the bearskin has an unusual silver plate.

112/15 Line Infantry, 32nd Regiment

The uniform of this Fusilier also follows the specifications of the White Uniform Regulations, and it even has the white metal buttons which are missing from the prior print. The silver shako plate and white cords are consistent with this latter detail. The use of a red pompom by a Fusilier is surprising, that colour normally being reserved for use by Grenadiers.

113/16 Line Infantry, Grenadier, 58th Regiment

This print depicts the standard dress of a French Line Grenadier during the Napoleonic era. The only detail which is arguably less than typical is the red cuff flap, since blue also seems to have been a colour used regularly for that feature.

114/169 Line Infantry, 100th Regiment

This Fusilier is wearing the 1812 model infantry jacket with lapels closing across the stomach to the waist and the characteristic below-the-knee gaiters typically worn with that style of coat. There are a number of surviving examples of the 'sunburst' style of plate on the shako of this figure, but none can be attributed to a particular regiment. There is another version of this print Type which labels the figure as representing the 130th Line Regiment. Note, once again, the use of a red pompom by a Fusilier and the lack of white piping around the cuffs and cuff flaps.

115/3.1 Line Infantry, Chasseur, 122nd Regiment 1809

The 122nd Line was formed on 1 January 1809 from personnel of the five Reserve Legions then being disbanded. The yellow collar and green epaulettes are standard Voltigeur distinctions (the 'Chasseur' terminology used in the caption of this print is obviously wrong), but the yellow cuff flaps are a particularly unusual feature. The white shako cords are also unusual, because green or yellow would be more logical colours in this context.

116/5.1 Line Infantry, [—] Regiment, Grenadier

This print complements No. 113/16 by depicting a line Grenadier in shako instead of bearskin. The shako plate shows the eagle decoration which is omitted in Type II Infantry prints. The brass edging to the shako visor is an uncommon detail, as is the white sword knot with red tassel.

117/16.1 Line Infantry, Fourrier

After 1808 every company of French infantry had one *caporal-fourrier*, or quartermaster-corporal, who was a senior non-commissioned officer entitled to bunk and mess with the sergeants of his unit. The only prescribed distinction for the uniform of this type of NCO was a single gold chevron on the outside of the sleeve above the crook of the elbow, but the evidence of this print suggests that the blue plume with red tip, the gold trim around the upper rim of the shako and the blue decoration on the collar were also approved badges of rank. The quartermaster-corporal otherwise wore the same uniform as the rank and file for his company.

118/111 Line Infantry, Sergeant-Major Planting an Eagle on a Redoubt

This fanciful print almost certainly was not intended to portray an actual incident, but it does convey a great deal of information about the 1804 model of French eagle and standard. Because the print does not depict a particular unit, the artist has left the wreaths in the corners of the flag either blank or filled with an imperial bee. The shoulder-strap indicates that this NCO belongs to a Fusilier company.

119/88 Line Infantry, Drum Major

It is very difficult to assess the accuracy of the uniform depicted in this print because there is no primary evidence that directly corroborates its most unusual features: the sky-blue coat, the lavish lace on the hat, the rows of lace across the chest, the crimson collar and turnbacks and the unique style of Hungarian knot decoration on the thigh of the breeches. Most surprisingly, the lace is silver instead of gold, which contradicts the normal rule of gilt distinctions for units with yellow metal buttons.

120/161 Line Infantry, Drummer Beating 'La Diane'

There are many verified cases of the adoption of elaborate uniforms for French Napoleonic drummers, but this print probably gives a good example of what the average level of ornamentation may have been. This Fusilier drummer is wearing the same basic uniform as his fellow privates, but it has been decorated with orange lace around the lapels and cuffs (but not the collar) and red 'swallow's nests' have been added at the end of the shoulder-straps. The red plume tipped medium blue is another decorative touch. This print also gives important primary evidence concerning the design and colours of French infantry drums.

121/201 Line Infantry Officer

This multi-subject print is weak both in terms of the basic engraving (note the lack of detail to the epaulets) and colouring (note the colour extending beyond the confines of the collar), but it does convey a great deal of useful information about officer's dress with the 1812 model uniform. The shako has more gold trim than one would expect for a junior officer (including the 'point up' chevron on the sides), especially in the austere times after the Russian campaign. The continued use of the gorget post-1812 is also unexpected. The riding-boots with brown cuff were popular footwear for an infantry officer who could afford his own horse.

122/224 Line Infantry on campaign, Sentinel

This picture presents a wonderfully atmospheric, if patently contrived, composition. The shivering Grenadier sentry has put a green leather case over his shako plume and has green gloves as well. His obvious source of warmth is his single-breasted overcoat, which in this case has a red collar. It is rather surprising to find him depicted as wearing white gaiters (instead of black) in winter.

123/237 Line Infantry, Corporal

The various distinctions of this NCO's rank have the effect of transforming the standard Fusilier uniform into something much more interesting. The black, tipped red, plume sitting atop a red pompom is unique in Napoleonic iconography, as is the diagonal drape of the white shako cord and the presence of a strip of white buttonhole lace (complete with button) on the collar. This print shows very clearly the tendency of most Martinet artists to depict the uniform shoulder-strap being held in place by a cross-strap of a contrasting colour. Note that this figure has no cuff flaps.

124/245 Military Scene

This bivouac print has an atypical background because very few tents accompanied the French armies on campaign. The Dragoon figure pulling the cape of his cloak up to his chin is particularly successful in conveying an impression of cold. The seated figure is a Fusilier private, but the details of the back of his uniform have not been provided. The dog defies classification unless it is an ill-groomed poodle.

125/249.1 Line Infantry, Sergeant

The uniform of this Fusilier sergeant holds no surprises except, perhaps, the fact that the cuff flap is red instead of blue (as specified in the 1812 Regulations). The gold trim on the upper rim of the shako and the blue-over-red plume are also noteworthy. The drill scene in the background provides a rare contemporary illustration of French soldiers in drill order wearing the 1812 model forage cap. An earlier state of this print shows the sergeant in a pre-1812 cut-away jacket.

126/263 Line Infantry, Fencing Master

This position does not appear in any official organisation charts of the French Army, but almost every regiment, including those of line infantry, had such an expert in its ranks to instruct his fellow soldiers in the noble art of swordplay. The Fencing Master would also represent his unit in duels of honour. The bicolor forage cap with two strips of white lace and a grenade ornament is noteworthy.

127/280.1 Line Infantry in 1813

This print provides a priceless rear view of the 1812 model infantry jacket, showing both the vertical pocket and the crowned 'N' ornaments in the turnbacks. The rear view of the shako is also instructive because it reveals the buckle used to adjust its fit. The colours of the shako *houpettes* (literally 'small tufts') indicate that the left-hand figure (violet tuft) belongs to the fourth company while his colleague (orange tuft) belongs to the third. Another, identical version of this multi-subject print bears the printed caption '*Garde Nationale, 1er Ban*'.

128/22 Light Infantry, Chasseur, 2nd Regiment, Voltigeur

The most striking features of this Voltigeur's uniform are the yellow plume with green holder, the yellow collar with white trim and the yellow shoulder-straps for the green epaulets. The basic template for this print does include cuff flaps, but they have been painted over in this instance. The white cords seem anomalous.

129/23.1 Light Infantry, Chasseur, [—] Regiment, Voltigeur From 1806 to 1814

The caption of this print is highly unusual because the hand-written notation certainly suggests that it was created in 1814 or later. More importantly, comparison with the preceding print reveals that this is a variant of the same print which has been reworked to remove the shako cords and change the cut of the jacket lapels to the 1812 model.

130/24.2 Light Infantry, Carabinier, (—) Regiment

This print provides one of the clearest primary source illustrations of the pre-1812 uniform of a Light Infantry Carabinier. The collar could have been trimmed with blue instead of white. Note that the gaiters do not have any elaborate trim around the top, a feature that is often shown in modern sources.

131/246 Light Infantry, Corporal

The uniform of this Chasseur Corporal has a number of unusual features. First, the cockade has been painted in such a way as to suggest that it was entirely of brass. Secondly, there is no other ornament or plate on the front of the shako. Thirdly, the shako cords are white. Fourthly, the jacket has pointed cuffs. The latter feature explains why real chevrons rather than straight strips of lace were used for the corporal's rank distinctions.

132/265 Light Infantry, Carabinier

A comparison of the uniform in this print with that in Print No. 24 provides a capsule history of the evolution of French military dress during the course of the First Empire because they depict the same notional uniform in both its pre- and post-1812 form. Since one of the main purposes of the 1812 Regulations was to cut down on expensive distinctions, it is curious to see that this figure still has a red band at the top of his shako and red trim on his gaiters. The four-button cuff flap is also noteworthy.

133/59 Artilleryman

One must doubt whether any Napoleonic line Artilleryman ever struck such a pose in action, but one must applaud the imaginative artistic license which accounts for the dramatic perspective of this print. In addition to showing accurately all the basic details of the French artillery uniform, this picture also provides unusual detail about French cannon and equipment such as the slow match used to fire the piece. Note the letter 'G' in the lower left-hand corner, identifying (presumably) Godissart de Cari as the artist.

134/60.1 Horse Artilleryman

The letter 'G' in the corner of this print is surprising because there seem to be notable differences in artistic quality between this and the prior print, which bears the same initial. The wearing of a busby by an artillery private is

difficult to explain, because there were no élite companies in the artillery to justify the expense of that item. It is perhaps significant in this regard that the majority of copies of this print that have been examined by the author show the figure wearing a shako with red reinforcing bands. The form of sabretache design is unusual and is not verified by any other primary source.

135/1 Line Infantry, Grenadier, 1st Regiment, Paris Guard

It is not surprising that a Paris publisher would choose to begin his series of prints with one depicting the uniform of the local civic guard, especially since the unit had played an honourable role in the 1807 campaign. The style of dress of the Paris Guard was identical with that of French line infantry, but its colours were unique.

136/1.1 Line Infantry, Grenadier, 1st Regiment, Paris Guard

All sources agree that the Paris Guard changed to a white uniform in 1808, with green facings for the 1st Regiment and red for the 2nd. The green facings were preserved when the two regiments were amalgamated into a single unit in 1812.

137/20 Line Infantry, 1st Regiment, Paris Guard

Like any line infantry regiment, this unit had Fusilier as well as elite companies. From 1807 until the adoption of the white uniform, these Fusiliers wore shakos with white cords.

138/160 Line Infantry, Chasseur, 1st Regiment, Paris Guard

A light infantry company was organised in each regiment of the Paris Guard in 1806, but the names for these companies may have changed from time to time and, moreover, may have been different between the two regiments. The green epaulettes with red crescents and the green shako cords of this figure are consistent with the 'Chasseur' designation used in the caption, but the yellow collar was generally used only by units designated as 'Voltigeurs'.

139/170 Line Infantry, Voltigeur, 1st Regiment, Paris Guard in 1810

The caption of this print uses the term 'Voltigeur' instead of the 'Chasseur' label used in the preceding print, which suggests that the 1808 reorganisation of the Guard may have resulted in some changes in this regard. The yellow collar and plume tip are consistent with the former terminology. Note that the bearskin does not have a plate.

140/243 Line Infantry Officer, 1st Regiment, Paris Guard

This officer does not appear to be either a Chasseur or Voltigeur type, so his yellow plume is inexplicable unless yellow was a centre company distinguishing colour.

141/14 Line Infantry, Chasseur, 2nd Regiment, Paris Guard

The original uniform of the 2nd Paris Guard Regiment was red with green facings, but the only Martinet prints depicting this unit known to the author illustrate the white uniform with red facings adopted in 1808. The uniform of this figure has the same company distinctions as the Chasseur of the 1st Regiment depicted in Print No. 138/160, but they show up more clearly against a white uniform background.

142/241 Line Infantry, Carabinier, 2nd Regiment, Paris Guard

This caption complicates the discussion of company designations in the Paris Guard by introducing still another variant. Nevertheless, the yellow collar suggests that the caption is wrong and that this figure represents a 2nd Regiment Voltigeur instead. Whatever the correct designation, the uniform is strikingly colourful. The cuff flaps appear to be white.

143/106 Light Cavalry, Dragoon, Paris Guard

The men of the mounted squadron attached to the Paris Guard wore Dragoon-style dress uniforms with the unique colour scheme of iron-grey with red facings. On the evidence of this print, the Paris Guard Dragoons were also equipped like line Dragoons.

144/17 Departmental Guard of Paris in 1808

From 1805 on, each French administrative Department was provided with a company of reserve conscripts to perform security tasks for the Departmental Prefect. The first uniform decreed for these Reserve Companies was sky-blue, with a variety of different facings (including white for the Department of the Seine encompassing Paris). There is another, near-identical state of this print in which the figure is wearing a jacket with lapels closed down to the waist, which could never have been the case because the sky-blue colour was abandoned years before the 1812-style jacket was adopted

145/126 Line Infantry, 1st Regiment, Departmental Guard, 1st Company

In 1808, Napoleon changed the basic colour of the Reserve Company uniform from sky-blue to white, and since the facings of the company from the Department of the Seine were already white, they had to be changed to sky-blue. There is no evidence that the soldiers of the Reserve Companies were entitled to any elite status, but the epaulets and sabre of this figure suggest this was true for (at least) the Departmental Guards of the nation's capital.

146/19 National Guard

In 1807, each cohort of the National Guard was divided into ten companies, including one of Grenadiers and one of Chasseurs. The only approved distinction for the latter units was the design of their buttons, but the evidence of this print suggests that the sabre and cross-belt (traditionally a perquisite of elite status) was adopted as well. The tricolor plume is unusual, as are the white metal buttons which create the most significant difference between this jacket and that of a typical Line infantryman.

147/127.1 Battalion of Chasseurs, residing at Flushing

This unusual unit was created in 1802 to provide a means of re-employing French soldiers who had served (as émigrés or otherwise) in foreign armies and who then (through desertion or otherwise) wanted to rejoin the French Army. As discussed at length in Section III(B) of the text, this print may be the least reliable of the entire series.

148/131 Line Infantry, 1st Colonial Battalion

The four Colonial Battalions of Napoleon's army were a repository for the least promising human material in the French military establishment, but, according to the evidence of this print, their uniforms were among the most colourful. This print provides the detailed information about facing colour and style which is missing from Napoleon's decree for the Battalions, which simply specifies that they will be dressed in iron-grey uniforms (iron-grey being in this case a distinctly bluish colour).

149/132 Line Infantry, Voltigeur of 1st Colonial Battalion

Given that the Colonial Battalions were essentially disciplinary units which were not sup-posed to have elite companies, it is startling to encounter this print of a spectacularly colourful Voltigeur of the 1st Battalion. Nevertheless, it seems hardly likely that Martinet would fabricate such a uniform, since its authenticity could easily be checked by his customers.

150/181.1 Officer of 1st Regiment of Volunteers of the Department of the Seine

The Volunteers of the Seine had only an ephemeral existence in the spring of 1814, but they probably did receive uniforms thanks to a personal expenditure of some 54,000 francs by their commanding officer, Colonel Jean Henri Simon. One wonders about the luxury of the bearskin busby, but the rest of the uniform seems very utilitarian. An alternate colouring of this print has a grey saddlecloth with red trim. An alternate version of Print No. 154 depicts an officer (in shako) of an infantry company attached to the Volunteers.

151/187 Imperial Customs Service, Foot Brigade

This and the following print about the Imperial Customs Service have unique iconographic value because, as indicated by the unusual artist's signature, they reflect information provided by an employee of the service itself. Although the Customs Officers were not (until the dark days of 1813 and 1814) expected to play a significant role in military affairs, their police function often led them into harm's way. This print confirms that they wore hats rather than shakos for most of the period.

152/188 Imperial Customs Service, Mounted Brigade

The uniform of this figure is remarkably fancy for a member of a para-military force. The horse furniture has distinct Hussar overtones, and the black sheepskin saddlecloth is highly unusual. Likewise, the amount and extent of lace trim seems lavish. Other reliable sources suggest that the vest should be green with white lace, as opposed to all-white.

153/21 Mounted Gendarme

The uniform of the mounted troops of the French Gendarmerie was distinguished primarily by a white aiguilette worn on the left shoulder. The right shoulder was supposed to be decorated only with a blue counter-epaulet, but this was eventually replaced in practice with the white trefoil shoulder-piece shown in this print.

154/261 Foot Gendarme

Although someone has taken pains to add the hand-written date of 1813 to the caption to this print, it seems to be a distinction without a difference because the versions of this print which lack that addition nevertheless illustrate the same uniform. The 1812 Regulations, which stress economy over perfection, specify the use of blue shoulder-straps for Gendarmes, but there is a consensus that the red epaulettes shown here were still commonly used.

155/275 Lancer-Gendarme

Starting in November 1810, the mounted squadrons of the special Gendarmerie created for service in Spain were re-uniformed and re-equipped as 'Light Horse' to make them more proficient in their appointed anti-guerrilla duties. The introduction of the lance was another manifestation of Napoleon's view that it was a weapon particularly suited for use in combat against irregular troops. This print is the only significant primary source illustrating the dress of these revamped units.

156/148 Line Infantry, Chasseur, Regiment of Isembourg

The unit formed by the Prince of Isembourg wore one of the most distinctive uniforms in the French Army during the Napoleonic Era. The basic colour was sky-blue, but it had a yellow collar, cuff flaps and piping. In this case, therefore, the yellow collar is a regimental norm rather than an elite company distinction. The plume and the epaulets, however, are certainly of Voltigeur origin.

157/268 Light Infantry, Chasseur, 3rd Foreign Regiment

Although it seems nearly certain that all facings on the first uniforms of the Irish Legion were yellow, it is equally well-established that the unit switched to green lapels and cuffs when the Legion was transformed into the 3rd Foreign Regiment in 1811. (The number on the shako plate indicates that this Print dates from that year or later.) The decorative impact of the green fringe of the epaulet is almost entirely lost against the similar background colour of the jacket.

158/243.1 Officer of Lancers, 9th Regiment, Elite Company

There is no real justification for the Polish dress adopted for the 9th Light Horse Lancers, since the regiment was actually created at Hamburg in 1811 through the amalgamation of two non-Polish corps – the 30th Mounted Chasseurs (French) and the Hamburg Civic Dragoons (German). Although the uniform shown in this Secondary Version print follows the specifications of the 1812 Regulations for this regiment, the unit in fact wore a green uniform with buff facings during the Russian Campaign and did not switch to this colour scheme until 1813. The outline of the decorative lace in the basic engraving (which is visible around the collar and lapels) has been correctly ignored and painted over by the colourist. That detail was relevant when this Type II Lancer Print was used for the officer of the Polish Guard Lancers in

Print No. 16/217, but it is not correct for this Line officer.

159/279 Lancer, 7th Regiment, Elite Company

The 7th Light Horse Lancers were simply the 1st Regiment of Lancers of the Vistula Legion operating under a new name, and they continued to wear the same Polish dress and yellow facings that they had worn since the unit's creation. One point of particular interest is the black plume with a medium blue tip. This figure is missing the wide white-and-blue striped waist belt specified by the 1812 Regulations. Note that the length of the lance causes the series title on this multi-subject print to be off-centre, and smaller than usual.

160/227 Portuguese Legion, Chasseur

The most distinctive features of the uniform of the Portuguese foot soldiers serving in the French Army were the brown coat and the unusual shako with raised front which was quite similar in design to the 'belgic' shako worn by the British Army at the end of the Napoleonic era. The uniform had other note-worthy features as well, however, including the unusual shape of the lapels, the absence of a cuff flap on the cuffs and the arrangement of the red trim on the white overalls. This Single Unit print is the most important coloured iconographic source of information about this uniform.

161/229 Portuguese Legion, Cavalry

The unique uniform of the Portuguese Legion cavalry is another type of dress which is known primarily because of the existence of the Martinet prints. It obviously differs a great deal from that of the Legion's infantry and, on the whole, is much less colourful, although the peculiar helmet provides a bold element. This print also gives a unique glimpse of the proper technique for using a carbine from horseback with the weapon still attached to the clip on the carbine shoulder-belt.

162/258.1 3rd Swiss Regiment, Grenadier

This print has the distinction of being one of the very few entries in the Martinet series that has an inaccurate caption, because the only Swiss Regiment with blue facings was the 2nd (the 3rd had black facings). The cut of the coat suggests a post-1812 date for this print, but bearskins had become a rare commodity by that time. The 1812 Regulations specify red piping for the facings, but none is evident here. They also specify red epaulets for the regimental Grenadiers, but the white ones in this print make more sartorial sense.